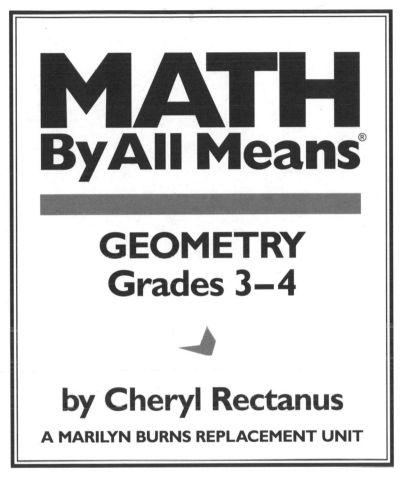

# MATH
## By All Means®

### GEOMETRY
### Grades 3–4

## by Cheryl Rectanus

**A MARILYN BURNS REPLACEMENT UNIT**

MATH SOLUTIONS PUBLICATIONS

**Editorial direction:** Lorri Ungaretti
**Art direction and design:** Aileen Friedman
**Typesetting:** Rad H. M. Proctor
**Page makeup:** David Healy, First Image
**Illustrations:** David Healy, First Image
**Cover background and border designs:** Barbara Gelfand

Marilyn Burns Education Associates is dedicated to improving mathematics education. For information about Math Solutions courses, resource materials, and other services, write or call:

Marilyn Burns Education Associates
150 Gate 5 Road, Suite 101
Sausalito, CA 94965
Telephone (415) 332-4181
Fax (415) 331-1931

**Distributed by Cuisenaire Company of America, Inc.**
**P.O. Box 5026**
**White Plains, NY 10602-5026**
**(800) 237-3142**

# MATH SOLUTIONS PUBLICATIONS
## A Message from Marilyn Burns

Teaching has always pushed my thinking, and my experiences teaching teachers at **Math Solutions** courses and workshops have deepened my understanding about the help teachers need for classroom instruction. To offer follow-up to **Math Solutions** inservice and further support teachers, I created **Math Solutions Publications** in 1987. Since then, we've published books in four categories, and the decisions we've made about what to write have been greatly influenced by specific requests teachers have made to me and other **Math Solutions** instructors. If you would like information about any of our books, or about our **Math Solutions** inservice, please call **Marilyn Burns Education Associates** at **1-800-868-9092**.

## Resource Books for Problem Solving

These books bring to teachers a vision of teaching mathematics through problem solving. They are professional teaching resources designed to stimulate, inspire, and support teachers as they work to translate the NCTM Standards into actual classroom instruction.

- *About Teaching Mathematics* by Marilyn Burns
- *50 Problem-Solving Lessons: The Best from 10 Years of Math Solutions Newsletters* by Marilyn Burns
- *A Collection of Math Lessons From Grades 1 Through 3* by Marilyn Burns and Bonnie Tank
- *A Collection of Math Lessons From Grades 3 Through 6* by Marilyn Burns
- *A Collection of Math Lessons From Grades 6 Through 8* by Marilyn Burns and Cathy Humphreys

## Linking Mathematics and Language Arts

The first book in the list below explains why students should write in math class, describes different types of writing assignments, and offers teaching tips and suggestions. The other three books show teachers how to use children's literature to introduce important math ideas to elementary students.

- *Writing in Math Class: A Resource for Grades 2–8* by Marilyn Burns
- *Math and Literature (K–3), Book One* by Marilyn Burns
- *Math and Literature (K–3), Book Two* by Stephanie Sheffield
- *Math and Literature (Grades 4–6)* by Rusty Bresser

## Math Replacement Units

Designed as an alternative to textbook instruction, each **Math By All Means** Replacement Unit presents a cohesive plan for four to six weeks of classroom instruction. The units focus on thinking and reasoning, incorporate the use of manipulative materials, and provide opportunities for students to communicate about their learning.

- ▪ *Math By All Means: Place Value, Grades 1–2* by Marilyn Burns
- ▪ *Math By All Means: Geometry, Grades 1–2* by Chris Confer
- ▪ *Math By All Means: Probability, Grades 1–2* by Bonnie Tank
- ▪ *Math By All Means: Multiplication, Grade 3* by Marilyn Burns
- ▪ *Math By All Means: Division, Grades 3–4* by Susan Ohanian and Marilyn Burns
- ▪ *Math By All Means: Geometry, Grades 3–4* by Cheryl Rectanus
- ▪ *Math By All Means: Probability, Grades 3–4* by Marilyn Burns

## Books for Children

For more than 20 years, I've brought my math message directly to children, beginning with **The I Hate Mathematics! Book,** first published in 1974. In 1994 I launched the Marilyn Burns Brainy Day Books series, linking children's literature and mathematics.

- ▪ *The Greedy Triangle* by Marilyn Burns
- ▪ *The King's Commissioners* by Aileen Friedman
- ▪ *A Cloak for the Dreamer* by Aileen Friedman
- ▪ *The $1.00 Word Riddle Book* by Marilyn Burns
- ▪ *The I Hate Mathematics! Book* by Marilyn Burns
- ▪ *The Book of Think* by Marilyn Burns
- ▪ *Math for Smarty Pants* by Marilyn Burns

# PREFACE

In the 1989–90 school year, Cheryl Rectanus was one of eight third-grade teachers from five schools in the San Francisco Bay Area to participate in a year-long project with Marilyn Burns Education Associates. Bonnie Tank and I created curriculum units for an entire year of math instruction for third graders and met with teachers monthly to present and discuss the units. With the endorsement of their principals, Cheryl and the other teachers in the project used the units to replace their existing programs.

Cheryl taught the original geometry unit, contributed to its revision, and in subsequent years taught later versions of it. This unit draws from Cheryl's three years of experience with the material. During this time, in addition to full-time teaching, Cheryl was studying for her master's degree at the University of California at Berkeley, immersed in research about constructivist learning. This unit gave Cheryl a way to blend theoretical studies with classroom practice, and she presents some of the research pertinent to children's learning of geometry in the introduction and appendix of this book.

Reading and editing Cheryl's manuscript was a particular pleasure for me for several reasons. First of all, I had taught the unit twice to third graders and was interested in comparing Cheryl's experiences with mine. At times, Cheryl's results and her interpretation of them matched my own experiences and, in that way, helped to confirm my beliefs. Other times, Cheryl's presentation offered me another way to look at a particular activity or at student's responses. All in all, her manuscript helped me view the unit from another perspective. It helped me think again about geometry, reconsider some of my own classroom instructional choices, and better understand some of the research that has been done about children's learning of geometry.

My hope is that the unit will help other teachers think about the potential and benefit of teaching geometry and learn how teaching geometry can contribute to their students' mathematical power.

The editing of the manuscript was an intense process for Cheryl and me. We talked about the educational issues, tinkered with the specifics of procedures, and considered what student work to include. After several months of working together on every aspect of the manuscript, we agreed to send it off to become typeset, designed, and printed. It's been typical for me at this stage of writing a book to be sure that I'll never again tackle such an enormous and detailed project. Cheryl felt similarly, but just recently, when I saw Cheryl at a math conference, she was renewed, refreshed, and thinking about writing another unit, this time for fifth grade, the level she's teaching now. So stay tuned.

All of the "From the Classroom" vignettes describe what happened when the unit was taught in a third-grade class. However, the grade level span assigned to the unit indicates that it is suitable for grades three and four. We've made this grade-level designation for two reasons. We know that in any class, there is typically a span in students' interests and abilities, and the activities in the unit have been designed to respond to such a span. Also, teachers who have taught the unit have found it successful with children in several grade levels and have reported that the activities are accessible and appropriate to a range of students.

Marilyn Burns
March 1994

# Acknowledgments

**Special thanks for the insight and support provided by the students, staff, and administrators with whom this unit was developed and tested.**

Many people contributed to the writing of this book.

I wish to express my gratitude to:

The students and colleagues with whom I've worked in the San Francisco Bay Area and in Portland, Oregon. Their insights and important questions contributed much to my professional development.

The consultants for Marilyn Burns Education Associates, whose high caliber of thinking about how children learn mathematics and how best to support that learning helped me refine my vision of a mathematics classroom where thinking, reasoning, and communicating are valued.

Marilyn Burns, for sharing her passion for learning through her writing, teaching, and conversations. Her profound respect for children and her commitment to students, teachers, and parents are extraordinary.

Lorri Ungaretti, for her patience, encouragement, and thoughtful attention to the many details of the publishing process.

Barbara and Karl Liechty, my parents, for their unwavering support and pride.

Fred Rectanus, my husband, who read and critiqued every draft. I'm grateful for his loving support and his willingness to head to the ski slopes or high desert with me when I needed a break. He is most appreciated.

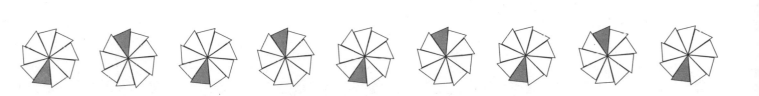

# CONTENTS

# INTRODUCTION

"Our next unit in math is about geometry," I told my class of 31 third graders. My self-contained class was part of a public elementary school of 375 children in a small city in the San Francisco Bay Area.

"What do you think geometry is?" I asked.

"Shapes," Jenny replied.

Drew added, "Geometry is all sorts of shapes and how you make them."

"It's part of math," said Emma.

Tanya said, "Geometry has to do with angles."

"Tell me about angles," I probed, hoping to find out what Tanya understood about them.

"They're the sides of a shape, where they meet," she replied, using her hands to help explain what she meant.

"I think geometry is designs that help you with math," Courtney stated.

Noah agreed. "It can be puzzles too, like the tangrams," he said. I had introduced the tangram puzzle to the class earlier in the year.

"I don't know that much about geometry," said Julie. "We didn't learn it much last year. Just names of shapes. We learned more about numbers." Several students nodded their agreement, and the class fell silent.

## Teaching Geometry in the Elementary Grades

Teachers and students often see geometry as an enrichment topic in the math curriculum. Textbooks reinforce this view by giving numerical concepts and skills the major emphasis and often placing geometry chapters near the end of the book. The implication is that geometry is something students should study after the dominant concepts of number and computation have been

"covered." Julie's comment about her mathematics learning last year was not surprising. The content of textbook lessons and standardized tests greatly influences classroom math teaching, as do pressures from parents who grew up learning mostly arithmetic in their elementary math classes.

I became particularly interested in the topic of geometry while studying for my master's degree and reading research about how geometry is taught to children, how children develop understanding about geometry, what assessment results reveal, and what the current recommendations are for mathematics teaching.

I learned that researchers have documented evidence indicating that some math programs do not provide sufficient opportunities for geometric problem solving and do not emphasize geometric content in ways that help students develop understanding (Battista & Clements, 1988). I learned that geometry is often taught by rote, with little emphasis on having students explaining their understanding (Fuys, Geddes, & Tischler, 1988). I found out that students who took the National Assessment of Educational Progress (NAEP) tests did best on assessments that asked them to identify common geometric figures and worst on those problems that required interpretation or application of geometric properties (Lindquist & Kouba, 1989).

I also read about the standards for teaching geometry recommended by the National Council of Teachers of Mathematics (1989). For kindergarten through grade four, the Standards specify a shift away from a focus on naming geometric figures and recommend the following:

"In grades K–4, the mathematics curriculum should include two- and three-dimensional geometry so that students can—

- describe, model, draw, and classify shapes;
- investigate and predict the results of combining, subdividing, and changing shapes;
- develop spatial sense;
- relate geometric ideas to number and measurement ideas;
- recognize and appreciate geometry in their world." (page 48)

The NCTM Standards also propose changes in methods of instruction and include the following list of instructional practices that need increased attention:

- Use of manipulative materials
- Cooperative work
- Discussion of mathematics
- Questioning
- Justification of thinking
- Writing about mathematics
- Problem-solving approach to instruction (page 20)

The rationale for these changes has been argued by several researchers (Davis, 1989; and Brown, Collins, & Duguid, 1989).

I studied the philosophy of constructivism, which stresses that children develop their own understanding through experiences that engage them actively in doing, thinking, and reflecting (Inhelder & Piaget, 1958, 1964; Vygotsky, 1962, 1978; and others). I also studied the van Hiele model of the

development of geometric thinking (van Hiele-Geldof, 1957; and van Hiele, 1986) and related this research to the NCTM recommendations. If you are interested in more information about constructivism, the van Hiele model, and the work of other researchers, see the appendix on page 143.

I was a full-time classroom teacher while studying for my master's degree, so I had the opportunity to apply what I was learning in my classroom. Teaching students daily provided concrete experiences that helped me connect the theories of research to actual classroom practice.

During this period I participated along with eight classroom teachers in a two-year project with Marilyn Burns and Bonnie Tank to implement a year-long third-grade curriculum organized into eight units. We met monthly, each time receiving inservice on a new unit and discussing our classroom experiences with the unit we had just taught. During the second year of the project, we met and talked about our experiences with the revised units. At the same time, 24 teachers in the Tucson Unified School District Chapter 1 math program were also teaching and discussing the units.

This geometry unit for third and fourth graders blends my experience in the two-year project with the research recommendations I studied in my master's program. The unit presents a teaching plan that encourages children to construct their own understanding of the mathematical concepts in geometry, builds upon students' existing understanding of geometry, and addresses the goals of the NCTM Standards.

## What's in the Unit?

In this five-week unit, students explore geometric ideas through a variety of developmentally appropriate problem-solving experiences in whole class lessons and independent "menu" investigations. The activities integrate ideas from the areas of logic, number, measurement, and patterns and also include art experiences and children's literature.

Children work with manipulative materials, interact with other students, and explain their thinking orally, in writing, and with pictures. Class discussions are a key element of the whole class lessons and menu activities. In discussions, children share their thinking, summarize and interpret results, listen to other students' ideas, and focus on the relationships and connections among concepts and activities.

Throughout the unit, students are actively engaged in constructing their own understanding rather than passively receiving rules and procedures. The students are primarily responsible for doing the thinking in the unit, while the teacher supports the children's thinking by developing an environment that encourages questioning, discussion among children, and intellectual risk-taking. Collaborative work in pairs and small groups supports the students' interaction.

## The Structure of the Unit

The unit is organized into four main areas: *Whole Class Lessons, Menu Activities, Assessments,* and *Homework.* In addition, the Children's Books section describes children's books that relate to the ideas in the unit. An appendix presents information about research that relates to geometry instruction. Blackline masters needed for the activities are included. A bibliography lists sources for research as well as children's books.

### Whole Class Lessons

Four whole class lessons, each spanning several days of instruction, introduce different geometry concepts to the children. These lessons provide a common set of introductory experiences on which the children can build their understanding of geometric ideas and vocabulary. Three lessons focus on explorations with two-dimensional shapes and the relationships among them; one lesson uses boxes the children bring from home to investigate three-dimensional shapes.

The instructional directions for each lesson are presented in four sections:

*Overview* gives a brief description of the lesson.

*Before the Lesson* outlines the preparation needed before teaching the lesson.

*Teaching Directions* gives step-by-step instructions for presenting the lesson.

*From the Classroom* describes what happened when the lesson was taught to one class of third graders. The vignette helps bring alive the instructional guidelines by giving an over-the-shoulder look into a classroom, telling how lessons were actually organized, how students reacted, and how the teacher responded. The vignettes are not offered as standards of what "should" happen but as a record of what did happen with 31 children.

### Menu Activities

The menu is a collection of activities that builds on the ideas presented in whole class lessons to provide children additional experiences with geometry. The menu tasks do not conceptually build on one another. Therefore, children do not have to complete them in any particular sequence. Rather, menu activities pose problems, set up situations, and ask questions that help students interact with the mathematics they're learning. Six activities are included on the menu. Four require the children to work in pairs or groups; two are designed for individual work.

The instructional directions for each menu activity are presented in four sections:

*Overview* gives a brief description of the activity.

*Before the Lesson* outlines the preparation needed before introducing the activity.

*Getting Started* gives instructions for introducing the activity.

*From the Classroom* describes what happened when the activity was introduced to one class of third graders. As with the whole class lessons, the vignette gives a view into an actual classroom, describing how the teacher gave directions and how the students responded.

For additional information about the menu system, see the introduction to the Menu Activities section on page 59.

## Assessments

The unit has four assessments. These differ from traditional paper-and-pencil tests in that students are encouraged to describe what they know and explain their reasoning. One assessment is suggested for the beginning of the unit and another for the end. The other two are recommended for the second half of the unit, after children have had experiences with geometric vocabulary and concepts. Assessments are no different in character than instructional activities. Teachers learn what their students understand through observation, by listening to children's comments during discussions, and from reading their written work.

For specific information about assessing understanding, see the introduction to the Assessments section on page 13.

## Children's Books

Children's books provide a way to integrate literature with math instruction. They can be a motivating way to extend students' understanding of geometric ideas and help them develop an awareness of geometry in their world. One children's book, *The Greedy Triangle* by Marilyn Burns, is an integral part of this unit. Other suitable books are described in the Children's Books section.

## Homework

Homework assignments have two purposes: They extend the work children are doing in class, and they inform parents about the instruction their children are getting. Suggestions for homework assignments and ways to communicate with parents are included in the Homework section.

## Appendix

The appendix presents information about constructivism and the work of Piaget, Vygotsky, and the van Hieles. It offers a background rationale for the activities in the unit.

## Blackline Masters

Blackline masters are provided for all menu activities and recording sheets.

## Bibliography

A bibliography is presented in two sections. One section lists the research references cited in the book; the other lists the recommended children's books and other books in the *Math By All Means* series.

# Notes About Classroom Organization

## Setting the Stage for Cooperation

Throughout much of the unit, students are asked to work cooperatively with a partner or small group. Interaction is an important ingredient for children's intellectual development. They learn from interaction with one another as well as with adults.

Teachers who have taught the unit have reported different systems for organizing children to work cooperatively. Some put pairs of numbers in a bag and have children draw to choose partners. Some assign partners. Some have seatmates work together. Others let children pick their own partners.

Some teachers have students work with the same partner for the entire unit. Others let children choose partners for each activity, allowing them either to change frequently or stay with the same person. Some don't have children work with specific partners but instead with the others who have chosen the same activity.

The system for organizing children matters less than the underlying classroom attitude. What's important is that children are encouraged to work together, listen to one another's ideas, and be willing to help classmates. Students should see their classroom as a place where cooperation and collaboration are valued and expected. This does not mean, of course, that children are never expected to work individually. However, it does respect the principle that interaction fosters learning and, therefore, that cooperation is basic to the culture of the classroom.

## A System for the Menu Activities

Teachers report several different ways for organizing the menu activities. Some teachers use a copy machine to enlarge the blackline masters of the menu tasks onto 11-by-17-inch paper, mount them on construction paper or tagboard, and post them. Although children are introduced orally to each activity, later they can refer to the directions for clarification. (Note: A set of posters with menu activity directions is available for purchase from Cuisenaire Company of America.)

Rather than enlarge and post the tasks, other teachers duplicate a half dozen of each and make them available for children to take to their seats. Mounting the tasks on tagboard makes the copies more durable. For either of the above alternatives, children take materials from the general supply and return them when they finish their work or at the end of class.

Some teachers prefer to assign different locations in the classroom for different tasks. For each activity, they place a copy of the task and the worksheets and materials needed in a cardboard carton or rubber tub. At the beginning of menu time, monitors distribute the tubs to the locations. The number of chairs at each location determines the number of children that can work there.

Each of these systems encourages children to be independent and responsible for their learning. They are allowed to spend the amount of time needed on any one task and to make choices about the sequence in which they work on tasks. Also, the tasks are designed for children to do over and over again, avoiding the situation where a child is "finished" and has nothing to do.

## How Children Record

Teachers also use different procedures to organize the way children record. Some prepare folders for each child, either by folding 12-by-18-inch sheets of construction paper or by using regular file folders, and require children to record individually even when working cooperatively. Some teachers prepare folders for partners and have the partners collaborate on their written work. Other teachers don't use folders but have students place their finished work in an "In" basket.

Some teachers have children copy the list of menu activities and keep track of what they do by putting a check by an activity each time they do it. Other teachers give children a list of the menu activities by duplicating the blackline master on page 130. It's important that the recording system is clear to the class and helps the teacher keep track of children's progress.

## About Writing in Math Class

For both learning activities and assessments, teachers must rely on children's writing to get insights into their thinking. Helping children learn to describe their reasoning processes, and become comfortable doing so, is extremely important and requires planning and attention. Experience and encouragement are two major ingredients.

It's important for children to know that their writing is important because it helps the teacher learn about how they are thinking. Teachers need to reinforce over and over again that the teacher is the audience for children's writing so the students need to provide sufficient details to make their thinking and reasoning processes clear.

For children who have difficulty with writing, it may be helpful at times to take their dictation or, as described several times in this unit, provide a tape recorder for them to use to explain their ideas.

## Managing Materials and Supplies

Teachers who have taught this unit report that they provided time at the beginning of the year for children to explore concrete materials they needed to use in their math learning. Also, all the teachers gave their students guidelines for the care and storage of materials. The following materials and supplies are needed for this unit:

### Materials
- Geoboards with rubber bands, one per pair of children
- Flat toothpicks
- Various size boxes with lids (The children bring these from home.)
- 9-x-12-inch envelopes
- Shallow paper cups
- Two-Color Counters with holes, Unifix Cubes, or other types of markers with holes in the middle of them
- Yarn, at least three different colors

**General Classroom Supplies**

■ Ample supplies of paper, including large sheets of newsprint or chart paper and construction paper
■ Letter-size envelopes, one per child, plus several extras
■ One shoebox
■ Scissors, at least one for each pair of children
■ Glue
■ Tape
■ Markers or crayons
■ Tagboard

In addition, recording sheets are specified for individual activities; blackline masters for these are included. Most teachers choose to have supplies of each sheet available for children to take when needed. Also, see the Children's Books section for information about the children's books that are suitable for the unit.

## A Suggested Daily Schedule

It's helpful to think through the entire unit and make an overall teaching plan. However, it isn't possible to predict how a class will respond as the unit progresses, and adjustments and changes will most likely have to be made. The following day-to-day schedule is a suggested five-week guide. It offers a plan that varies the pace of daily instruction, interweaving days for whole class lessons with days for independent work on menu activities. The schedule also suggests times for discussing menu activities and giving homework assignments.

Class discussions of menu activities are included throughout the day-to-day plan. These are typically scheduled several days or more after the menu activity is introduced, giving children time to experience the activity before being asked to participate in a class discussion. Since students will be working on menu activities at their own pace and completing them at different times, it's important to check with children about their progress. At times, you might mention to children that they'll be discussing a particular activity the next day and should be sure to work on the task so they can contribute to the discussion. Although times for class discussions are suggested in the plan, use your judgment about when it's best to have them. For general information about the importance of class discussions, see the Menu Activities introduction on page 59. For suggestions about how to conduct specific discussions, check the "From the Classroom" section in each menu activity.

The Children's Book section (see page 121) presents books that relate to the geometric ideas in the unit and are suitable for reading to the class. One of these books—*The Greedy Triangle*—is used for a whole class lesson and is included in the daily schedule. However, the schedule does not mention times for reading the other books; choose those you wish to read and when to do so as the unit unfolds.

**Day I**      **Assessment: What Is Geometry?**
**Whole Class Lesson: The Four-Triangle Problem**

Elicit responses from children about geometry and then have them record their ideas in writing. After children have completed the assessment, begin Part 1 of *The Four-Triangle Problem* whole class lesson.

**Day 2**      **Whole Class Lesson: The Four-Triangle Problem (continued)**

Continue with the whole class lesson, having children search for four-triangle shapes.

**Day 3**      **Whole Class Lesson: The Four-Triangle Problem (continued)**

Allow time, if needed, for children to continue their search for four-triangle shapes. Introduce Part 2 of the whole class lesson and organize the shapes into a class chart.

**Day 4**      **Introduce Menu Activities: Same and Different, Rotating Designs**

Present the directions for the menu activities *Same and Different* and *Rotating Designs*. Students choose one of the activities to work on for the remainder of the class. Give homework assignment: *Polygon Search*.

**Day 5**      **Menu**

Begin class by having the children report their experiences at home doing *Polygon Search*. List their findings on a chart. Then review the directions for the two menu activities and let students work on the menu.

**Day 6**      **Whole Class Lesson: The Greedy Triangle**

Read and discuss the book *The Greedy Triangle*. Give students the assignment of writing their own stories.

**Day 7**      **Menu**

Students work on menu activities or continue writing their geometry story. Leave time at the end of class for one or two children who have finished their stories to read them to the class. (Note: Continue having a few children share their stories each day.)

**Day 8**      **Introduce Menu Activity: Four-Triangle Color Arrangements**

Begin class with a class discussion about *Rotating Designs* and have students try to match templates with designs. Then present the directions for *Four-Triangle Color Arrangements*. Students choose a menu activity to work on for the remainder of the class.

**Day 9**      **Menu**

Students continue work on the menu activities. Ask children who haven't yet done so to work on *Same and Different,* so they can participate in tomorrow's class discussion about the activity. Give homework assignment: *Rotating Designs*.

**Day 10    Menu**

Begin class by asking the children to report their experiences at home doing *Rotating Designs*. Post the designs. Then students work on menu activities. Use the second half of the period for a discussion of *Same and Different*.

**Day 11    Whole Class Lesson: Toothpick Patterns**

Introduce Part 1 of the lesson and have children make designs. If there is time, begin a discussion of the students' findings.

**Day 12    Whole Class Lesson: Toothpick Patterns (continued)**

Finish the discussion of the students' findings. Introduce Part 2 of the lesson. Students make their decks of toothpick playing cards.

**Day 13    Whole Class Lesson: Toothpick Patterns (continued)**

Teach the rules and have the children play the toothpick game.

**Day 14    Introduce Menu Activity: The Put-in-Order Problem**

Present the directions for *The Put-in-Order Problem*. Students choose menu activities to work on for the remainder of the class.

**Day 15    Menu**

Students continue work on the menu activities. Direct children who haven't yet done so to work on *Four-Triangle Color Arrangements*, so they can participate in tomorrow's class discussion about the activity.

**Day 16    Assessment: Polygon Cards**

Begin class by discussing *Four-Triangle Color Arrangements*. Then present the *Polygon Cards* assessment. When children complete their polygon cards, they choose a menu activity to work on for the remainder of the class.

**Day 17    Introduce Menu Activity: Square Up**

Begin class by having children discuss their strategies for *The Put-in-Order Problem*. Then present the directions for *Square Up*. Also, if you wish, add *Polygon Cards* to the menu so that children can try to guess what's on the back of one another's cards.

**Day 18    Whole Class Lesson: Investigating Boxes**

Introduce Part 1 of the *Investigating Boxes* whole class lesson. The children choose and compare boxes.

**Day 19    Whole Class Lesson: Investigating Boxes (continued)**

Introduce Part 2 of the *Investigating Boxes* whole class lesson and have students sort boxes. If there is time, introduce Part 3.

**Day 20**   **Whole Class Lesson: Investigating Boxes (continued)**

Continue with Part 3 of the *Investigating Boxes* whole class lesson. Students trace all the faces of a box onto large paper and attempt to match one another's boxes and tracings. If they have time, students choose a menu activity to work on for the remainder of the class.

**Day 21**   **Introduce Menu Activity: Covering Boxes**

Present the directions for *Covering Boxes*. Students choose activities from the menu to work on for the remainder of the class.

**Day 22**   **Menu**

Begin class by having students discuss their strategies for playing *Square Up*. If you wish, after the discussion they can write about their strategies. Then students continue work on the menu activities. Give homework assignment: *Square Up*.

**Day 23**   **Assessment: Box Riddles**

Begin class by having the children report their experiences at home playing *Square Up*. Then present the directions for the *Box Riddles* assessment activity. When students finish writing their riddles, they choose a menu activity to work on for the remainder of the class.

**Day 24**   **Menu**

Students continue work on the menu activities. If you wish, add *Box Riddles* to the menu. Also, have a class discussion about *Covering Boxes*.

**Day 25**   **Assessment: What Is Geometry? (Revisited)**

Ask students to discuss and record in writing their ideas about geometry. (You may want to have them first read their assessment from Day 1.) If they have time, students choose a menu activity to work on for the remainder of the period.

## A Letter to Parents

Although parents learn about their children's experiences from homework assignments and papers sent home, you may want to give them general information about the unit before you begin teaching it. The sample letter on the next page informs parents about the goals of the unit and introduces them to some of the activities their children will be doing.

Dear Parent,

In our next math unit, we will explore geometry. Studying geometry is important for children, as it helps them broaden their idea of mathematics beyond the study of numbers and connect mathematics to the real world. To build their spatial abilities, children will manipulate, compare, describe, and sort two- and three-dimensional shapes.

The language of geometry will be used throughout the unit. Your child will learn many geometric terms including quadrilateral, trapezoid, parallelogram, pentagon, hexagon, polygon, rectangular prism, angle, parallel, and congruent.

The children will be engaged in a variey of problem-solving activities to help develop their understanding of shapes and the relationships among them. They will search for different ways to make polygons by arranging four triangles. They will investigate patterns made from four toothpicks placed either end-to-end or at right angles. They will examine the properties of various boxes and compare and sort them in several ways. They will learn several geometric games that involve them in thinking strategically as well as spatially.

It is important for children to relate the geometry ideas they're learning at school to the world around them. From time to time, they will be asked to find specific shapes at home to report to the class. Also, they'll be asked to bring in boxes for our exploration of three-dimensional shapes.

I encourage you to talk with your child about what he or she is learning. Please feel free to visit our classroom at any time.

Sincerely,

## A Final Comment

The decisions teachers make every day in the classroom are the heart of teaching. Although this book attempts to provide clear and detailed information about lessons and activities, it isn't a recipe that can be followed step-by-step. Rather, the book offers options that require teachers to make decisions in several areas: sequencing activities, organizing the classroom, grouping children, communicating with parents, and dealing with the needs of individual children. Keep in mind that there is no "best" or "right" way to teach the unit. The aim is for children to engage in mathematical investigations, be inspired to think and reason, and enjoy their learning.

# CONTENTS

# ASSESSMENTS

Assessing children's understanding is an ongoing process. In the classroom, teachers learn about what students know from listening to what they say during class discussions, observing and listening as they work on independent activities, having conversations with individual children, and reading their written work. From a collection of observations and interactions, teachers gain insights into children's thinking and reasoning processes and learn about children's mathematical interests and abilities.

In the area of geometry, third graders are typically familiar with the names of basic geometric shapes but do not fully understand the properties of these shapes and how they relate to one another. Traditional geometry assessment focuses on having children recognize and name shapes, often emphasizing terminology instead of understanding. Assessment in this unit has a different goal: to help teachers assess students' spatial abilities and understanding of geometric relationships.

Four assessments are suggested. *What Is Geometry?* given at the beginning of the unit has students discuss what they think geometry is and then record their thoughts in writing. In *Polygon Cards* children create their own polygon cards to reveal what they have learned about polygons. In *Box Riddles* children write geometry riddles, a task that involves children with describing a three-dimensional object using measurement and two-dimensional geometry. Finally, for *What Is Geometry? (Revisited)*, children reread their papers from the beginning of the unit and write again about what they know about geometry.

Many opportunities also exist throughout the unit for informally assessing students' understanding. Teachers can learn about students' understanding of geometric ideas and vocabulary through observing both their contributions to class discussions and their interaction with other students in pairs and small groups.

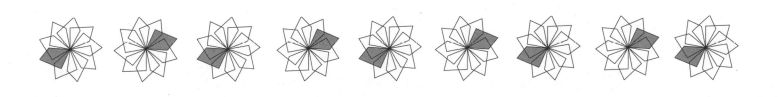

# ASSESSMENT  What Is Geometry?

**FROM THE CLASSROOM**

Many third graders are familiar with geometry because shapes are a visible part of our world and because they learned about it in earlier grades. Despite prior experience, however, many children do not have a comprehensive understanding of geometry concepts and vocabulary.

For this assessment, tell the students that over the next month they will be learning about geometry, and you are interested in learning what they already know about it. Listen to all ideas offered without judging or correcting; the goal of the discussion is for you to collect as much information as possible about the range of understanding among the children.

After everyone who wants to has offered ideas, ask the students to write down what they already know about geometry. This assignment gives you a chance to learn the thinking of all the children, whether or not they volunteered ideas during the discussion. The children's writing will give you a base from which to compare their thinking at the end of the unit.

"For the next five weeks we'll be learning about geometry," I told the children. "What do you think geometry is?"

After students had expressed their ideas, I asked them to write about what they already knew about geometry. I explained that they would read these papers again at the end of the unit and write again about what they had learned.

The children's writing revealed a range of understanding about geometry. Julie, for example, wrote: *I dont no about gomrty xsept shaps. I like nubers bettr.*

Tanya seemed to have a more complete view of geometry. She wrote: *Geometry is shapes and angles and sizes. You have geometry in your house. Your bed is a shape (rectangl) and cookies are round. And my sister said you have angles on shapes.*

I could often count on George to offer an opinion on most subjects, but he had remained silent during the discussion. On his paper, he wrote: *it can be fun and it can be borring but I like it. it pretty much it can be like art in numeres ways. it...it really you no how many shapes are in the world infinity!!!! thats all I no.*

Grant hadn't offered any ideas during the discussion either. He wrote: *I don't think I'll ever understand "geometry."*

Elena, who was often vocal about her dislike of numbers, wrote: *I prefer shap's better then number's because numbers are sort of difficult for me. I like shap's because you can do so meny thing's with them.*

# CONTENTS

# WHOLE CLASS LESSONS

The unit includes four whole class lessons. Each lesson introduces students to a different way of investigating shapes.

In the first lesson, *The Four-Triangle Problem,* children cut four triangles from squares of construction paper and investigate ways to arrange them into other shapes. Later, the class organizes the shapes into a graph and discusses their mathematical names.

The children's book *The Greedy Triangle* provides the context for the second whole class lesson. The book's illustrations and appealing story present many ways that shapes appear in our world. After hearing and discussing the story, students write geometry stories of their own.

In *Toothpick Patterns,* the third whole class lesson, students arrange toothpicks into patterns, use those patterns to make playing cards, and play a game that calls for spatial sense and strategic thinking.

*Investigating Boxes* is the fourth whole class lesson. Students investigate three-dimensional shapes by examining boxes, comparing their similarities and differences, and sorting them by various properties.

The lessons in the unit provide many opportunities for children to explore shapes. They also introduce children to standard geometric vocabulary: triangle, rectangle, square, trapezoid, quadrilateral, pentagon, hexagon, parallelogram, congruent, and more.

It's best to intersperse whole class lessons with menu activities. Introducing some menu activities early in the unit provides students with options when some finish whole-class-lesson work earlier than others. (See "A Suggested Daily Schedule" on pages 8–11 for one possible day-by-day plan.)

# WHOLE CLASS LESSON   The Four-Triangle Problem

## Overview

This two-part lesson introduces students to geometric concepts and vocabulary, including triangle, quadrilateral, square, rectangle, parallelogram, trapezoid, pentagon, hexagon, and polygon. Children have the opportunity to see different shapes in relation to one another and to learn about diagonals, angles, parallel lines, and congruency. The lesson provides children with experiences sorting and classifying shapes, helps students develop their spatial reasoning abilities, and encourages flexible thinking.

The lesson requires several math periods. In Part 1, students cut four triangles from 3-inch squares of construction paper and investigate ways to arrange them, following the rule that sides that touch must be the same length and match exactly. In Part 2, the class organizes the four-triangle shapes into a graph and learns their mathematical names.

Three menu activities extend the children's experience with the four-triangle shapes. In *Four-Triangle Color Arrangements* (see page 77), the children investigate possible two-color arrangements for the four-triangle shapes. In *Same and Different* (see page 62), pairs of students choose two of the shapes and investigate their similarities and differences. *Rotating Designs* (see page 68) uses the four-triangle shapes for art designs and provides experience with rotational symmetry.

## Before the lesson

Gather these materials:
- ■ Approximately 300 3-inch construction paper squares of two contrasting colors (Avoid red and green together, in case you have color-blind students.)
- ■ 18-by-24-inch newsprint, one sheet for each pair of students
- ■ 9-by-12-inch envelopes, one for each group
- ■ Two sheets of chart paper, one entitled "Geometry Words" and one left blank
- ■ Scissors
- ■ Tape

## Teaching directions

### Part 1: Searching for Four-Triangle Shapes

■ Post the chart paper entitled "Geometry Words" so it's available to begin a class list of geometry vocabulary. Distribute the 3-inch squares so that each group of children has a stack of about 20 of each color. Have additional squares available.

■ Explain to the students that they will make shapes from construction paper triangles. Show how to fold and cut a square in half on the diagonal to make two triangles. Have each student cut a square demonstrated. Pose the problem of finding all the different ways to put the two triangles together, following the rule that sides that touch must be the same length and match exactly. Model the rule by showing several ways to put triangles together that do and do not follow the rule.

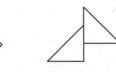
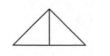

This is okay.                    These are not okay.

Ask students to work in groups and tape together each shape they find.

■ Discuss the three possible shapes: square, triangle, and parallelogram.

If groups find only one or two of the possible shapes, show the others and have students build them with their triangles. This is a good opportunity to name the parallelogram. It's also a good time to start the class Geometry Words list on the chart paper. Write: "square," "triangle," "parallelogram," and "diagonal." You may wish to make a sketch on the chart to illustrate each word.

It's common for students to make two of one shape, usually the parallelogram, and think they are different because they are positioned differently. Show children how to test for congruency by rotating and flipping to see if two shapes match. Introduce the word "congruent" and add it to the Geometry Words chart.

■ Pose *The Four-Triangle Problem.* In groups, children try to find all the possible arrangements using four triangles, two of each color, and tape together the four-triangle shapes they make. In each arrangement, each triangle must touch the side of at least one other triangle and follow the rule that sides that touch must be the same length and match exactly. (Note: There are 14 possible noncongruent shapes. Do not give this information to the class; instead, ask students to try to find as many as they can.)

■ Circulate among the groups. When a group tells you it has found all the possible arrangements, ask students to explain how they know. If you notice that a group has duplicate shapes, explain that you see some that are the same and ask the group to find them. If students in a group have not found all 14 possibilities, tell them to keep looking. Continue the investigation during one or two more math periods, as long as the students sustain interest. Do not expect all groups to find all 14 possibilities. They'll find out which ones they're missing in Part 2 of the lesson. Finally, label the chart "Polygons."

## Part 2: Sorting the Four-Triangle Shapes

■ In a second lesson, sort the four-triangle shapes into rows on a class graph. Rule the blank chart paper into four rows. Tell the children that they'll bring up shapes one by one, you'll post them in the correct row, and they will try to figure out how you're sorting them. (Sort the shapes according to the number of sides and angles they have, using the first row for triangles, the second for quadrilaterals, the third for pentagons, and the fourth for hexagons.)

If a child has a theory about how you are sorting the shapes, ask him or her not to tell but to bring up a shape and post it in the correct row. Also, when children post shapes, have them check by rotating and flipping to be sure that their shapes aren't congruent to one already posted. (Note: For later activities, each group will need a complete set of shapes, so as children contribute shapes to the class graph, direct them to make replacements for their group collections. Also, tell groups to make any shapes posted on the class graph that they hadn't found.)

■ When all 14 shapes have been posted, have children share their ideas about your sorting system. After a discussion, write the labels you used: triangle, quadrilateral, pentagon, hexagon. Finally, label the chart "Polygons."

**NOTE** A class list of geometric terminology can help students become familiar with the standard language of geometry and provide a reference for discussions and writing assignments. However, children become comfortable with these words only through many opportunities to hear and use them in context over time.

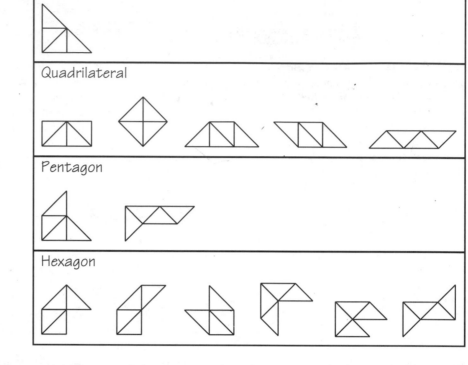

Add the new shape names to the Geometry Words chart and, if you wish, make sketches. Also, discuss the names of the different quadrilaterals: square, rectangle, parallelogram, and trapezoid. Add new names and "polygons" to the class Geometry Words chart.

■ For an extension, borrow a set of four-triangle shapes from one group and sort them into two shape groups—with and without at least one right angle. Have the class guess your system. (Note: Students most likely aren't familiar with the term "right angle." It's typical for them to say "square corner" or something else to describe a right angle. Accept their language and, if you wish, introduce the standard name.) If there is time, have groups explore other ways to sort the 14 shapes.

**NOTE** Polygons are shapes with straight sides that enclose an interior region. Polygons are classified by the number of sides and vertices they have:

Triangle – 3
Quadrilateral – 4
Pentagon – 5
Hexagon – 6
Heptagon – 7
Octagon – 8
Nonagon – 9
Decagon – 10

# FROM THE CLASSROOM

## Part 1: Searching for Four-Triangle Shapes

Before beginning the lesson, I assembled tape, scissors, and 3-inch squares of blue and green construction paper. The students in my class sit in groups of four children, and one child at each table has the job of "Group Supplies Person." It's his or her job to get the materials for everyone in the group; rarely do I distribute anything myself. I asked the children in charge of supplies to gather them.

I then began the instructions. "We'll be making shapes in this activity using the 3-inch squares of blue and green construction paper," I told the children. Holding up a blue square, I said, "I'm going to fold and cut this square on the diagonal." I indicated what I meant by "diagonal" by point-

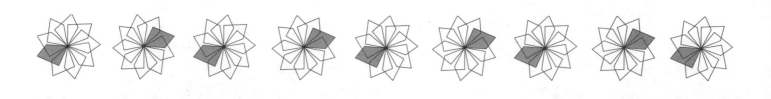

ing to one on the square. I didn't define the term, instead allowing children time to develop understanding of the word in context.

"What shapes will I have after I've cut the square?" I asked. Almost every hand in the room shot up.

"When I count to three, quietly say your answer aloud," I told the class.

"Triangle," was the unanimous reply. I directed the students' attention to the chart paper entitled "Geometry Words." I wrote the words "square," "triangle," and "diagonal" on the chart and drew sketches to illustrate each.

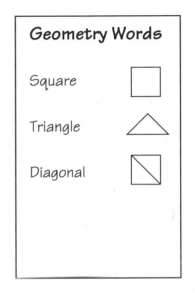

Then I folded and cut the square.

"Your first job is to fold and cut a square on a diagonal and put the two triangles back together to make a square," I said. I was interested in the students' spatial visualization abilities, so I scanned the class as they followed my direction. After a minute or so, most of the students had put their triangles together to make squares. I asked them to help anyone having difficulty at their table.

"Your second task," I explained, "is to make a different shape with your two triangles. The shape must follow this rule: Only sides of the same length can touch, and they must match exactly." I modeled the rule by demonstrating with two triangles how to place them correctly and incorrectly.

"Once you do this, compare your shape with the others in your group. Decide if your group has found all the possible shapes that can be made following this rule, and how you know. Tape your shapes so they won't fall apart when you hold them up." The problem of finding different arrangements is a spatial visualization task; deciding when they've found all possible arrangements is a logical reasoning task.

The students began to work. I observed until the majority of students had completed the task. After five minutes, I called for the children's attention. I could tell that most of them felt they had found all the possible arrangements because the conversations had shifted from math to what was going to happen after school.

"Who can describe a shape they made so that I can draw it on the board?" I asked. Several children raised their hands, and I called on Kendra.

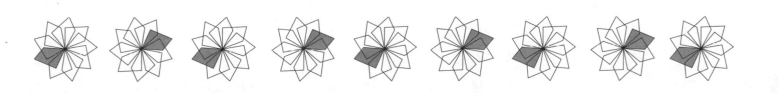

"Well, I took the back of one triangle and put it up to the back of another triangle, like this," she said, and she held up her parallelogram for the class to see. Eight or nine children raised their hand and called out, "I made that too."

"The shape that Kendra made has a name," I told the class. "Does anyone know what it is called?"

Four suggestions were offered. "Rhombus." "Trapezoid." "Diamond." "Parallelogram." I knew that my students had had many experiences in earlier grades using Pattern Blocks, and their former teachers had used the vocabulary the children mentioned.

"The shape is a parallelogram," I said, adding the word to the class chart.

Lisa commented that she wanted to compare her shape with Kendra's to see if it was the same.

"Go ahead," I told Lisa. To the class I said, "Sometimes you can rotate or flip a shape so that it fits exactly on top of another. Mathematicians have a word to describe that. They say that the shapes are congruent." I wrote "congruent" on the chart. "Whenever you want to check to see if your shape is congruent to another, please do so."

"Did someone make a different shape?" I continued. Tanya volunteered.

"I made . . . well, it's a . . ." Tanya stopped. Justin leaned over and whispered in Tanya's ear. "Justin will tell you," Tanya said. "It's too hard to say in words." Justin took over.

"She made a bigger triangle from the two smaller triangles," he said. "She put them back to back but didn't flip one like Kendra did." Justin is facile with language and can be counted on to contribute to class discussions. I drew Tanya's shape on the board.

"Did anyone else make a triangle like Tanya's?" I asked. A third of the students nodded or raised their hands in agreement.

"I found another shape," announced Alex. "It's a square." He held it up to show the class, and I added his shape to the others on the board.

"Did anyone find a different shape?" I asked again.

Edward raised his hand. "I found a diamond," he said.

"That's not a diamond, it's a rhombus!" Noah exclaimed vehemently.

"No, it's not a diamond or a rhombus," insisted Alex. "It's a square that you turned just a little bit."

The room buzzed with conversation. I hadn't anticipated this and wanted to pursue the issue further to learn about the students' understanding.

"Take a few minutes and discuss with your group what you think a square, a diamond, and a rhombus are," I instructed the children. "Then be prepared to make an argument to your classmates to convince them of your reasoning." I ask children to provide a rationale for their answers to help them understand that I'm interested in their thinking as well as in their answers.

Four students immediately headed over to the Pattern Block buckets and returned to their seats with blue and tan blocks. The conversations were lively, as the children spent several minutes trying to convince one another of their reasoning.

"What do you think?" I asked after five minutes had passed.

Cal began. "A SQUARE, A DIAMOND, AND A RHOMBUS ARE THE SAME THING!!!" he shouted as loudly as he could. He pounded on the table for emphasis. A few children giggled, and I was taken aback, until I realized how Cal had interpreted my instruction to "make an argument."

"Not that kind of argument, Cal," Tanya said, and Cal smiled sheepishly.

"Why do you think the shapes are all the same, Cal?" I asked.

"Actually, I don't really know yet," he responded.

I called on Kendra next. "Well," Kendra answered, using her hands again to demonstrate what she meant, "I think Edward's shape is like a square that's been pulled out of shape."

Noah again burst into the conversation. "It has to be a rhombus because if you take the blue rhombus from the Pattern Block bucket and hold it up to the tan diamond, which I think is a parallelogram, the shapes look the same but they're different sizes, so the shape *has* to be a rhombus!" It's typical for children to confuse mathematical language when they're learning.

Justin said, "I think a diamond is just a square that's been rotated a little bit. And a rhombus is a square that's been stretched. It doesn't have square corners like a square does. So a rhombus doesn't have square corners and a square does. That's the difference between the two. Edward's shape has square corners, so it must be a square."

The conversation continued for about five more minutes. I was struck by the high level of engagement: Every student was contributing to the conversation in some way. Some students spoke to the whole group, while others swiveled in their seats to face the child speaking or nodded their heads when they heard a viewpoint with which they agreed. Still others whispered to their table mates about something someone had said. I was also impressed by how much the children had to offer about their understanding of geometry.

I asked for the students' attention again, and told them that their thinking was very interesting to me. I shared that I was comfortable with their confusion about the issue and explained that their discussion was like those that mathematicians might have, posing an idea and then making arguments to convince others of their thinking.

Justin eagerly waved his hand and interrupted, "But what do your math dictionaries say those shapes are?" Justin knew that I kept in the classroom two dictionaries of mathematical terms. We referred to them often.

I read aloud the definitions of square and rhombus, realizing that they weren't very helpful for the majority of the children. Also, I drew a sketch of each shape on the board. I didn't push further, but explained that we would be working on many activities over the next few weeks to help the class understand more about geometric ideas.

I then asked if anyone had found a different shape. No one responded, and Sara finally said, "I took the triangles and tried them in as many ways

**NOTE** Not all children are comfortable sharing their thinking aloud in front of the whole class. They can participate in other ways, however, by listening or talking with others in small groups. It's important to validate a variety of ways a child can contribute to a discussion.

**NOTE** It's best to introduce correct geometric terminology in the context of learning activities in which children have concrete references and opportunities to hear the standard language used. Definitions of terms should connect to and evolve from classroom experiences.

as I could, but all I came up with were the same ones as everybody else. So I don't think there are any more."

"I agree with Sara," Nichole said. All but one or two children nodded their agreement. I added "rhombus" and "diamond" to the chart. Even though diamond isn't a standard mathematical term, it came from the students and I felt I should acknowledge it.

### Introducing the Activity

"What you'll do now is work with your group to find all the shapes that can be made from four triangles, two blue and two green. Like the problem we just worked on, the sides must touch, and the sides that touch must be the same length." I demonstrated what I meant with four triangles.

"Start by cutting one of each color square on the diagonal. Compare arrangements in your group to be sure you're finding different ones. Tape your shapes so that they'll stay together when you hold them up later for others to see. What questions do you have?" I asked.

Justin said somewhat hopefully, "Knowing you, I bet you aren't going to tell us how many shapes there are, are you?"

"No," I said. "I'd like you to grapple with that for a while." The emphasis in this activity is not just on finding all the shapes but also on students figuring out how they know they've found all the shapes.

### Observing the Children

The children eagerly began work. They cooperated well with one another, sharing materials and space. I didn't have to clarify directions because students asked one another when they had questions. We had spent time early in the year learning what it meant to "ask everyone at your table before you ask an adult." Students learned that we had 31 teachers in our room and that they would need to learn to rely on themselves and on one another as well as on me. The children had had many opportunities to work together and share a limited number of materials throughout the year, and now, in January, their experience was paying off. I could spend my time moving around the classroom observing each group, asking questions, and informally learning as much as I could about the students.

Mark and his group organized their work by spreading out the shapes they had made so they could look at them as a group and check for congruency. "I made this one. Did anyone else make it?" was a comment I overheard frequently.

After about 40 minutes of work, Tom's group called me over.

"We think we've found them all," said Tom. As I scanned their 12 shapes, I noticed a congruent pair of shapes.

"I see two congruent shapes," I told the group. "After you find them . . ."

"Oh, there they are," Tom interrupted. Tom has strong spatial skills, and I wasn't surprised that he quickly discovered the two shapes.

"Keep looking for other shapes," I finished, moving away.

"Okay, guys, back to the drawing board," I heard Tom say as I went over to another group.

**NOTE** Students probably won't find all the possible shapes or be able to explain why they thought they had found all of them. Typically, third graders are not able to devise a strategy for systematically exhausting all possibilities. This is an example of one difference between how children and adults think.

Emma told me, "We think we've found them all because we've worked for almost 45 minutes, and we haven't found a new shape for the last 15 minutes."

As I glanced at their shapes, I saw that they had made 12 shapes, 2 of which were the same. "Check for congruent shapes," I told the group.

By the end of class, several groups had decided they'd found all the shapes (although I determined by a quick count that they hadn't). Others were not convinced. I gave each group a 9-by-12-inch envelope for their shapes and told them they could continue the investigation the next day.

The children spent math time the next day searching for all the shapes; some continued their search on a third day. I was impressed with the sustained interest in the problem. It seemed just right for them. The students actively folded and cut paper squares, manipulated shapes, talked with one another, and moved freely around the room. I noticed that some children needed to check each new shape for congruency by physically matching it to those already made, while other students could mentally rotate or flip a shape to decide.

Some groups did find all 14 shapes. I found that I didn't need to suggest further explorations for the early finishers. The children had learned since the beginning of the year that I expected them to pursue their own extensions, and we had talked about what this meant and modeled it in detail. One group pretended its shapes were puzzle pieces and tried to fit them into the shape of a rectangle. Kendra and Courtney decided to explore all the shapes that could be made with five triangles. Other students were happy to draw faces on their shapes, particularly those children for whom the group task had been particularly challenging.

### A Class Discussion

On the third day, I called the children together for a class discussion. "I'm curious to know whether any groups think they've found all the possible shapes," I said.

Almost all the children raised their hands. Nicole began. "We found 14. We don't think there are any more because every time we think we have a new shape, it's just like one we already made!"

Emma explained, "In our group, we searched for half a day and only found 2 more shapes. Now we have 14, and we haven't found another since yesterday. So I'm definitely convinced that we have them all."

Ben said, "We found 15. We looked for a long time. I think that when you don't find a lot after a while, you know you're getting close." Others looked surprised. Tom went over to look and found that Ben's group had two pairs of congruent shapes. "So you only have 13," he said.

Jenny said, "After looking for two days, we're only finding doubles. So we're convinced that there are 14. Even if we worked for two more hours, we wouldn't find one!"

"Are there 14?" Justin wanted to know.

"Yes," I told him. The groups that had found 14 cheered.

"Don't worry if your group didn't find all 14 shapes," I said to the class. "You'll have a chance to see which ones you missed in the next activity, and you can complete your set."

## Part 2: Sorting the Shapes

I posted the chart paper ruled into four rows. "One person at a time will contribute a shape, and I'll post it on this chart." I explained. "I won't tell you how I've chosen to sort them. You'll have a chance to examine the shapes and guess." My plan was to sort them by the number of sides and angles each shape had. The first row was for triangles, the second for quadrilaterals, and the next two for pentagons and hexagons.

As children brought shapes to the bulletin board, I posted them in the correct rows. I instructed the children to make duplicates of any shapes they brought to the board so that each group had a complete set of shapes. I also told the children that if someone brought a shape to the bulletin board that their group hadn't made yet, they were to make that shape and add it to their set. The class studied the chart intently as it took form. Frequently children brought a shape up to the graph to check to see if it was congruent to one already there.

"Finally," I finished, "if you notice that you have some congruent shapes, remove the extras, so you have exactly one of each shape for your group."

When the graph had all but 3 of the 14 shapes on it, I asked the class if anyone yet had a theory about how I was sorting the shapes. About a third of the students raised their hands.

"Don't say your idea aloud yet, but each time someone brings up a shape, hold up one, two, three, or four fingers to indicate the row in which you think it belongs," I instructed the children. I pointed to each row as I counted.

Felicia brought me the rectangle next, and children held up different numbers of fingers. I told the children to whisper to one another about where they thought the rectangle should be placed and why.

"Would anyone like to share an idea?" I asked.

Gordon came up to the board. "All these on the bottom row, if you put a mirror on them they would have this line, s . . . sip . . . it starts with a 's,' and if you fold the shape the two halves match exactly, so the rectangle goes there." he said.

"Do you mean the ones in the bottom row have a line of symmetry?" I asked. Gordon nodded.

"But they don't," Alex interjected. "Look at the one that looks like the state of California. It doesn't have symmetry." He got up, took down the shape, and folded it in half. It wasn't symmetrical. We hadn't studied symmetry before, and I was curious about what Alex and Gordon knew. I opted to continue the discussion, however, rather than interrupt the children's thinking to satisfy my curiosity.

"Oh yeah, you're right," Gordon said and sat down.

Emma shared her idea next. "I think the first one is a triangle, the second row is all rectangles and squares, so the rectangle goes there. The bottom row is all shapes that represent something, like the cat, the fox, the state of California," she finished.

George said, "I think it goes in the second row too, but look, there's a rocket ship in the third row."

"Emma and George are correct about where the rectangle goes," I told the children. "Who else has a theory about how I sorted the shapes?"

Craig raised his hand and said somewhat tentatively, "The ones in the third row have five corners."

"Can you show us what you mean by that?" I asked Craig, and he came to the board and carefully counted the corners of each pentagon.

Jenny said excitedly, "All the ones on the bottom row have six corners!" She came up and counted them.

"I think that's it!!" George called out.

Kendra added, "And in the second row they all have four corners."

"So it goes 3-4-5-6 corners," said Timmy triumphantly, as the class shouted with excitement.

After the class calmed down, we placed the remaining shapes on the graph, and I continued the discussion.

"Shapes with three sides and three corners have a special name," I told the class. "Does anyone know what it is?"

"Triangle," replied David. His tone of voice indicated I had asked an obvious question. I wrote "triangle" on the first row of the graph.

"What about shapes with four sides and corners?" I continued.

"Squares?" Kendra asked.

"It can't be," Jenny said. "They've not all squares." The class was silent for a moment. "Quadrilaterals?" suggested Jenny.

"Yes," I replied, and wrote the word next to the quadrilaterals. I added it to the Geometry Words chart, having the students say it aloud softly as I wrote it.

"And shapes with five sides and corners?" I continued.

More silence. Jenny spoke up again. "Pentagons?" she said.

"Yes, shapes with five sides and corners are called pentagons," I replied, writing the word next to the pentagons and also on the Geometry Words chart.

"What about these?" I asked, indicating the hexagons.

"Hexagons!" Maurice and Noah cried out simultaneously, prompting Alex to remark, "We didn't make a pattern block hexagon. I wonder if you can make one?"

"I don't think so," said Courtney confidently.

I added hexagon to the Geometry Words chart and then I talked with the children about the different quadrilaterals, naming the square, rectangle, parallelogram, and trapezoid and talking about their characteristics. I mentioned that a square was a special kind of rectangle, with all sides the same length, and a rectangle was a special kind of parallelogram, with all square corners.

Several students asked what shapes with 7, 8, 9 and 10 sides were called, and I gave the names: heptagon, octagon, nonagon, and decagon. I added all these names to our chart. Finally, I said that all the shapes we had created were called polygons, and I labeled the graph we had created by writing "Polygons" at the top. The children seemed interested in the new words and talked about them with one another, as I gave each group an envelope for their four-triangle shapes.

On subsequent days, I gathered the class on the rug under the bulletin board, borrowed one group's set of shapes, and sorted the shapes in different ways. I didn't make permanent records of these graphs but merely placed the shapes into groups and had students guess my rule. The rules I used were: shapes with right angles and shapes without right angles, shapes with at least one line of symmetry and shapes without a line of symmetry, and shapes with dents (concave shapes) and shapes without dents (convex shapes).

**NOTE** A quadrilateral is a four-sided polygon. Parallelograms are quadrilaterals with opposite sides parallel and equal. Rectangles are parallelograms that also have equal angles (all 90°). A rhombus is a parallelogram with four equal sides. A square is a rhombus with equal angles; thus, a square is also a rectangle. Finally, a trapezoid is a quadrilateral with two parallel sides.

# WHOLE CLASS LESSON   The Greedy Triangle

## Overview

This lesson connects a mathematics activity with a language arts experience. After hearing the children's book *The Greedy Triangle* read aloud, students write their own versions of the book or make up their own geometry stories. Writing a geometry story requires each child to provide his or her own context for the vocabulary and concepts in the unit. It also helps you learn more about how students see geometry as a part of the world around them.

## Before the lesson

Gather these materials:
■ *The Greedy Triangle* by Marilyn Burns (See Children's Books section, page 123.)

## Teaching directions

■ Read aloud *The Greedy Triangle* by Marilyn Burns. This book tells the story of a triangle who became dissatisfied and went to a local shapeshifter for another side and angle. Although life as a quadrilateral improved, the triangle soon became dissatisfied again and returned to the shapeshifter for another side and angle. The triangle kept asking for more sides and angles, eventually running into new difficulties and finally deciding to return to being a triangle. The story presents many ways shapes appear in our world.

■ After reading and discussing the story, tell the children that each of them is to write a story. Students can either retell *The Greedy Triangle* or make up a geometry story of their own. They may include illustrations if they wish.

■ Invite volunteers to share their stories with the class. Class discussions of the children's writing can focus on many things—geometry concepts or vocabulary, the elements of stories, what the writing reveals about students' lives, geometry shapes in the world, or whatever you or your students are interested in pursuing.

## FROM THE CLASSROOM

"I have a geometry story to read to you," I explained to the class one morning. "It's called *The Greedy Triangle* and is about a triangle who was dissatisfied with life and continually yearned for more." The children listened carefully while I read the book, at times making comments to one another.

"Wow!" said Timmy, when I finished. "Imagine if it lived in San Francisco. Then it would crash into cable cars!" Timmy was referring to the part of the story in which the triangle has so many sides and angles that it can't keep its balance and rolls down a hill, crashing into fences and trees, colliding with bicycles, and terrifying walkers. Several children sitting nearby laughed at Timmy's comment and began rolling and bumping into each other. I brought them back to order.

"I'd love to be a triangle!" Kendra said enthusiastically. "I'd be a sail on a sailboat!"

Justin added, "I'd rather be a circle. Then you'd be more useful!"

"Close your eyes for a moment," I said to the children. "Imagine the greedy triangle as it got more sides and more corners. Imagine what it looked like with many sides and corners."

The children closed their eyes and the class was quiet. I waited a bit and asked them to open their eyes. "What did you see?" I asked.

Emma began. "Well, if it had lots of sides then they couldn't be very long. So what I saw was a circle rolling all over the place." Several students began giggling and again rolled into one another on the rug.

"Me too!" George shouted. "Can I draw it on the board?"

I quieted the children and nodded to George. He came to the board and drew a shape that had many sides and corners and looked somewhat circular. Many students nodded in agreement when he was finished, saying, "Yeah, that's what I saw too."

"A circle isn't made of sides and corners," I told the class. "Instead, a circle is a smooth path with every point on the path the same distance away from a point in the middle." I drew a dot on the chalkboard and, taking a piece of string about six inches long, I held one end on the dot I had drawn and pulled the string taut. With chalk, I drew a path where the string reached, making a circle.

Timmy raised his hand. "Wouldn't you get the same thing with very, very short lines?" he wondered.

"Actually, you would *approach* the shape of a circle," I replied, "but you'd never actually make one. The shape would appear to be a circle, but it actually would still be a polygon because it was made with many sides and angles."

### Introducing the Activity

"Right now," I then explained, "you'll each begin to write your own geometry story. If you want, you can retell *The Greedy Triangle* or write a story like it. Or, you can make up your own story about a triangle or another shape. Or, if you'd rather, you can make a book about all the things a triangle can be and illustrate it."

Elena asked, "Can we copy the story you just told us?"

Gena responded, "She just said we could, Elena!"

"Can we take it home and publish it?" Courtney asked.

"Sure," I said.

Justin asked, "Does a certain thing have to be in the story? Does the triangle have to be greedy?"

"The story has to involve geometry," I responded. "It will help me understand what you know so far about geometry and how you relate it to the world around you."

"Can we work with a partner?" Felicia disliked writing.

I replied, "It's fine to talk about your story with someone else, but I want you to write your own story."

### The Children's Stories

The stories the students wrote were interesting to me for several reasons. I learned about students' views of how geometry is part of the physical world around them. I gained insights into what some children understand about the structure of stories. Most importantly, I learned more about my students' lives and thoughts.

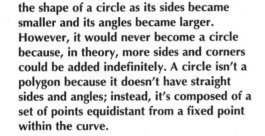

**NOTE** The greedy triangle approached the shape of a circle as its sides became smaller and its angles became larger. However, it would never become a circle because, in theory, more sides and corners could be added indefinitely. A circle isn't a polygon because it doesn't have straight sides and angles; instead, it's composed of a set of points equidistant from a fixed point within the curve.

CHAPTER 1 THE GREEDY TRIANGLE

Once upon a time there was a greedy triangle. He wanted everything — more sides — more corners — to be a Hexogon — to be a Quadrilataral — to be a pentogon — to not be a polygon — to not be a triangle — everything.

CHAPTER 2 THE GREEDY TRIANGLE WISHES

One day the Greedy Triangle made a wish. he wished that he had one more side, and one more corner. The Greedy Triangle turned in-to a Quadrilataral! He wasn't a Triangle any more!

CHAPTER 3 THE GREEDY TRIANGLE GETS HIS WISH

The Greedy Triangle wished agan, and the same thing happened. The Greedy Triangle has 3 sides and corners.

Courtney wrote her story in four chapters.

THE LAST CHAPTER

The Greedy Triangle kept wishing, and finaly he had so many sides, that he suddenly started colling and rolling, and he couldn't stop.

EPOLOG

The triangle kept rolling, and know one even saw him agan.

THE END

4

About half of the students chose to retell *The Greedy Triangle*, varying the story somewhat. For example, Timmy wrote: *Once upon a time there was a Greedy square and he always wanted more. One night he glued a point on and the next night and the next and the next and the next until he turned into a decagon. The next morning he looked at himself and tried to think of what he could be but he couldn't. For the next year he pulled off all his points until he was a triangle and was a pennant for the Boston Red Sox and tried to be happy.*

When he was working on the story, Timmy came to me and asked if I had any idea where a decagon was used in the world. I wasn't able to think of an example. I suggested that Timmy sketch different shapes with 10 sides and see if his sketches suggested something in the real world.

Cal patterned his story after *The Greedy Triangle* and included a reference to Pattern Blocks, which he loved to use. He wrote: *Once there was a traingal who was walking down Wildwood Ave when he saw a hexogon, the hexgon said·hi and the tringal said hi and at the same time he was thinking about how much fun it wood be to be a hexogon, so he wished & wished & wished. So he went home and had a bath.*

*When he woke up he felt really wierd he took a bath and the water turned yellow. he looked at him self and scremed HOLY TALETO! he was a butuful yellow hexagon. he was so excited he splashed water everywhere!*

*Soon he got bored of being a hexogon, and wanted to be a cricle and so he wished and wished and he was a cricle. And the next day he triped and rolled down a hill. A car was parking all of a sudden . . . help I'm going 52 miles pher hour!*

*BAM crunch. the cicrle wanted to be a tringle agian and the 2nd day he was in the hospital he truned into a tringal. the end.*

Mark's story, "Sometimes Six Is Better than a Dot," was a reversed version of *The Greedy Triangle*. He wrote about a hexagon that kept wishing for fewer sides until it became just a line and finally a dot. Mark's writing showed his difficulty remembering how to begin and end sentences. He wrote: *Once there was a hexagon. So was his friends and mom and dad. one day he wanted to see what it was like to be a pentagon, So he went to the jeany. he rubbed it. He was a pentagon he liked being a pentogon for a little bit. Then he wanted to be a quadreladeral so he went to the wishing well he was a quadreladeral. He got tired of being a quadreladeral so he wanted to be a triangle. He was and he liked it for a little bit. Then he didn't he wanted to be two sides cunected. He was he liked it kind of but now he does not. He wants to be a line. He is and his friends think he is crazy so do his family. He wants to be a dot. He is he hates it. He liked being a hexagon the best. He was a hexagon. then he went up insted of down. He still liked being a hexagon. He was not crazy after all.*

Emma wrote about a square named Sam: *There once was a square named Sam. Now let me tell you about his personality. Sam never made up his mind and Sam also was VERY GREEDY. When Sam the square got anything he never gave it back! Now after being a square for 22 long years he decided to use a feather which a magic bird had givven to him. So he took the feather out of it's case and started to think about a good wish. I think I'll whish to be a pentagon, said Sam. So he was a pentagon for two years. then he wanted to be a hexagon, then a heptagon, octogon, decagon. After that he ate and ate and ate intill he was so fat he could not eat one thing or els he would explod. Be he ate one more plate. BOOM! that was the end of him.*

A few students chose to talk about what triangles can be in the world. Julie, for example, wrote: *A triangle can be a building. A triangle can be part of an A. A triangle can be part of a star or part of a sail boat. A triangle can be a part of the golden-gate-bridge. A triangle can be a lader. A triangle can be a tent.*

Tanya made a book. On each page she wrote one thing that a triangle could be and included an illustration. Each illustration clearly showed how a triangle could be part of the object. She wrote: *The triangle could be a sign, a rocket, or a hat, or some paper, or a ramp, or a jungle jim, or a triangle, or a kite. The end.*

Some students' stories gave insights into their feelings. Nicole's story, for example, centered around the sad dodecagon's effort to make friends, reflecting Nicole's own difficulty in this area. Drew wrote about a pentagon named Kevin who had no other pentagons to play with. When the pentagon found a friend and went fishing, Drew wrote: *Alex felt good to have a friend even though they weren't friends for a long time.*

A few students' stories told me about their own interests but didn't include much reference to geometry. Craig, for example, wrote about a square who wanted to go on vacation to see a football game, referring to a "square bowl" instead of a "super bowl."

Gena wrote a silly story without much of a geometric basis. Her story was about a foolish square who wanted to become a circle and wound up becoming a barrel for applesauce. Then he wished to be a square again, and had applesauce all over him. Gena ended her story: *He went to the well and washed himself off. Then he wished that he was home again. That's the end.*

Tom titled his story *The Triangle Who Was Never Satisfied* and used a good deal of dialogue—something new for Tom. His story had a gruesome ending; after turning into a piece of pizza, the shape was eaten!

Tom entitled his story "The Triangle Who Was Never Satisfied."

A Geometry story The Triangle who was never satisfied

Once upon a time there was a triangle who stayed on the wall in a class room and never did any thing but stay, so one day the triangle said, "I've had it!" and left. So then he was a sail on a sail boat and he liked that so much! He thought that was so very cool awsome! Until one day he said, "I've had it" and left. Next he was a Christmas tree and he thought that was so awsome. He also liked getting all the pretty lights and glass balls but after Christmas he said, "I've had it," for the 3rd time and left. Then he was a pizza slice and was bought and right before he was eaten he thought how nice it would be if he was back on the wall in the class room, then he was eaten.
The End
The reason why he stopped liking everything was becase every thing got boring.

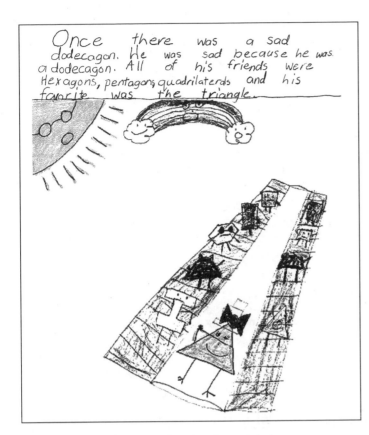

Once there was a sad dodecagon. He was sad because he was a dodecagon. All of his friends were Hexagons, pentagons, quadrilaterals and his favorite was the triangle.

Nicole illustrated her story, showing the sad dodecagon as the letter "I."

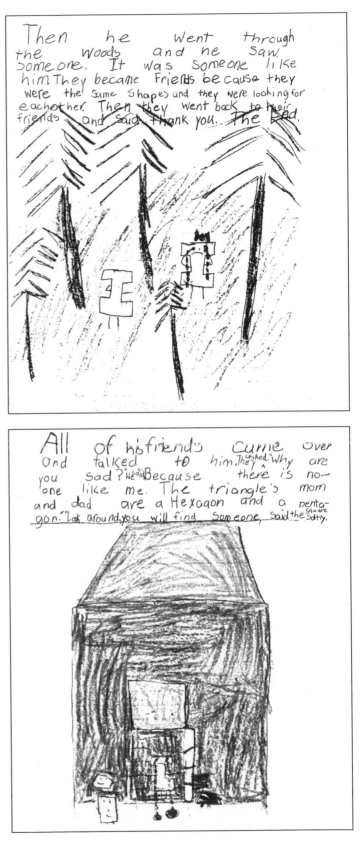

Then he went through the woods and he saw someone. It was someone like him. They became Friends because they were the same shapes and they were looking for eachother. Then they went back to their friends and said thank you. The End.

All of his friends came over and talked to him. They asked, "Why are you sad?" He said, "Because there is no one like me. The triangle's mom and dad are a Hexagon and a pentagon." "Look around, you will find someone," said the square. Softly.

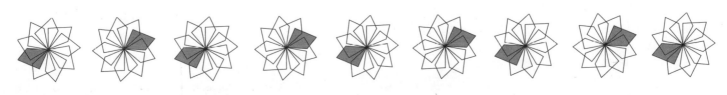

Julie wrote about where triangles appear in the world.

> ## What can a triangle be?
>
> A triangle can be a building. A triangle can be part of an A. A triangle can be part of a star or part of a sail boat. A triangle can be a part of the golden-gate-bridge. A triangle can be a lader. A triangle can be a tent.

## A Class Discussion

Students were interested in hearing one another's stories, and almost everyone wanted to read his or her story aloud or have me read it aloud to the class. Children listened carefully and offered specific feedback about the strengths of the writing as well as suggestions for improvement.

For example, after Timmy shared his story, Ben began the discussion about it. "I liked your story, Timmy," he said. "I had a good picture in my mind of the shape pulling off the points and trying to be happy." Several children murmured agreement.

"But you might tell us more about your shape," continued Nichole. "I mean, we don't know much about him so it makes the story . . . well . . . kinda boring." Timmy looked hurt.

"I don't think it's boring," Edward quickly said. "I like the idea. Maybe you could tell us why he wasn't happy."

Timmy squirmed uncomfortably and said, "Well . . . I don't know why he wasn't happy."

George brightly suggested, "Maybe he was fat and ugly and nobody liked him."

Nicole replied in a disgusted voice, "That's not very nice, George."

"Well, neither was your comment about the story being boring," George quickly shot back.

Maurice spoke up, saying, "There are lots of reasons in stories for why characters are unhappy. We could help you if you wanted us to, Timmy."

Timmy continued to look somewhat uncomfortable and grumbled, "I thought we were supposed to be talking about geometry in the story, not about the characters."

"You're right," said Emma, who was an avid writer, "but you want to make the story interesting." Emma had a keen sense of audience. She continued, "Sometimes it takes me a while to figure out what I want the characters to be like in a story. Your ideas are good, so it wouldn't be too bad fixing the story. I could help you. Maybe we could do it on the computer."

"Okay," Timmy acquiesced. He loved using the computer.

"And we could all try to help figure out what things a decagon could be!" added Justin.

**NOTE** Deciding when to end an investigation for a class discussion is one of the many classroom decisions that requires professional judgment. It's important to allow enough time for students to participate and contribute to a class discussion but not so much time that they lose interest.

Some students were more enthusiastic than others about incorporating suggestions, and the discussion went on for another 20 minutes. I felt it was worthwhile because the children focused on elements of story as well as on geometry concepts. The dialogue among students about the stories was rich and enthusiastic.

I stopped the discussion when some of the children lost interest. Over the next several days, some students continued to write geometry stories during writing time, and I made time for them to read their stories to the class.

# WHOLE CLASS LESSON Toothpick Patterns

## Overview

This two-part lesson helps develop students' spatial reasoning abilities and provides experience with congruence, mirror symmetry, and rotational symmetry.

In Part 1, students investigate all the ways to arrange four toothpicks by placing them end-to-end so they form either straight lines or right angles. In Part 2, children make a set of cards with the toothpick patterns and use them to play a game that calls for spatial sense and strategic thinking.

The menu activity *The Put-in-Order Problem* (see page 89) extends the *Toothpick Patterns* lesson by having the students solve a problem related to the game they learned in the whole class lesson.

## Before the lesson

### Part 1: Arranging Four Toothpicks

Gather these materials for each group of four students:
- Flat toothpicks, about 80 (Note: Be sure to get flat toothpicks, as they can be easily glued to paper.)
- White glue
- Shallow paper cups for the glue
- Approximately 24 6-by-9-inch sheets of construction paper, a different color for each group

### Part 2: The Toothpick Game

Gather these materials for each group of four students:
- 1 to 2 sheets of toothpick dot paper (See Blackline Masters section, page 139.)
- Scissors
- Four 5-by-8-inch index cards
- Markers or crayons
- One rubber band

## Teaching directions

### Part 1: Arranging Four Toothpicks

■ Explain to the children that they will work in groups to find all the different ways to arrange four toothpicks, following two rules:

> 1. Each toothpick must touch the end of at least one other toothpick.
>
> 2. Toothpicks must be placed end-to-end either in a straight line or to make square corners.

■ Tell students they will glue each arrangement to a separate sheet of 6-by-9-inch colored construction paper by dipping both ends of each toothpick in a cup of white glue and pressing the toothpick in place on the paper.

■ Ask a volunteer to suggest one possible arrangement. Make the suggested toothpick arrangement and demonstrate how to glue the toothpicks to the construction paper. Repeat for a second arrangement.

■ Explain that if a shape can be rotated or flipped to match another shape, both shapes are congruent and count as the same. Show how to test for congruence by drawing a shape on a sheet of newsprint and rotating and flipping it to see if it matches another shape. Demonstrate how holding the paper up to a window makes it possible to see the drawing when you turn the paper over. If the word "congruent" isn't already on the Geometry Words class chart, add it.

■ As groups work, circulate and observe the approaches students take to solve the problem. If you notice a group has made congruent shapes, tell the children but don't point out the shapes; leave them the problem of finding out which shapes are the same. As groups report they have found all the arrangements, discuss with them why they think so. Rather than telling children that there are 16 possibilities, ask them to keep looking and figure out some way to be sure they have found all the possibilities.

■ For a class discussion, have one group post its toothpick patterns. Number the patterns so the class can more easily refer to them in discussion. Ask the other groups to compare their patterns to the ones posted and see if they have any others to add. This process should produce all 16 patterns, but if not, show the class which are missing. Finally, have all groups label their arrangements, using the same numbers you did, and create any patterns they are missing. (Note: There is no significance to the numbering of the patterns; it's just important that all the children use the same numbers for ease of communication.)

## Part 2: The Toothpick Game

■ In a second lesson, have each group make a deck of 16 playing cards, one for each of the toothpick patterns. Students transfer the 16 toothpick patterns onto toothpick dot paper and cut them apart. They fold four 5-by-8-inch index cards in quarters along the lengths and widths and cut them along the fold lines to make backs for the cards. They then glue each toothpick pattern to a quarter of the index card and decorate the backs of the cards to make a matching deck.

■ Introduce the game. You need one group's deck of cards and four toothpicks. Choose three children to play the game with you. Explain that the object of the game is for all group members to play all of their cards. Group members take turns, but they need to work together in order for the group to succeed.

■ Model how someone in the group first chooses a card, makes the pattern with the toothpicks, shuffles the card back into the pack, and then deals all the cards so each player has four. (Groups of three or five don't shuffle the beginning card back into the deck, but leave it face up on the table and deal the rest of the deck so that each player has the same number of cards.)

■ To play, the students place their cards face up in front of them so that everyone in the group can see them. The first player places a card next to the toothpick pattern on the table, following the rule that the pattern on the card can be made by changing the position of just one toothpick in the pattern on the table. The player then moves one toothpick so that the pattern of the toothpicks matches the pattern on the card.

■ Players take turns placing a card and moving a toothpick, each playing a card with a pattern that can be made by changing the position of just one toothpick in the last pattern put down.

■ Encourage children to help one another with moves and discuss the patterns. If someone can't play a card, he or she says, "I pass." If all group members play all their cards, the group has won. Sometimes, however, groups reach a point where no one can play another card; when this happens, it's a stalemate.

■ After students have played the game enough times to be able to discuss strategies, initiate a class discussion. Raise the following questions: "Can all the cards be played in every game, or can you get stuck?" "Are some cards easier or harder to play? Why?" "What's a 'good' card to start with?"

■ After a class discussion, have students write about the strategies they used to play the game.

# FROM THE CLASSROOM

## Part 1: Arranging Four Toothpicks

"With your group, you're going to investigate patterns that you can make with four toothpicks," I told the class seated on the rug. I had assembled the materials we would need for the activity. I placed four toothpicks on the overhead projector.

"The four toothpicks must be arranged following two rules," I said. "One rule is that each toothpick must touch the end of at least one other toothpick. The other rule is that the toothpicks must either touch end-to-end in a straight line or make square corners." I arranged the toothpicks on the overhead projector to make a square and asked, "Who can explain why this shape follows the rule?"

Tanya raised her hand. "They all touch and they make square corners," she said.

"What about this?" I asked, as I arranged the toothpicks into a shape that looked somewhat like a "w."

Immediately Edward said, "It doesn't work, 'cause the ends don't make square corners."

"And they're not in a straight line," Kendra added.

"Think about another pattern that follows the rules," I said, "and talk to your neighbor about it. In a minute I'll ask someone to build his or her suggestion on the overhead, so we can all see it." The students began to talk to one another.

After a minute or so, I called for the children's attention. "Who would like to share an idea with the class?" I asked. About two-thirds of the class volunteered, and I called on Timmy.

"You could make a straight line, like this," Timmy said, arranging four toothpicks on the overhead projector.

**NOTE** Discussions in small groups allow more children to express their ideas than whole class discussions do. Also, some students find talking in small groups less threatening than sharing their ideas with the whole class.

He continued, "It works, because you said they have to make a straight line or be like a square corner, and this one has the ends touching in a line." Others nodded their agreement.

"You've seen two toothpick patterns," I said, "the square and the line. Your group task is to find all the possible toothpick patterns. When your group builds a pattern that you agree fits the rules, glue the arrangement onto a 6-by-9-inch piece of construction paper." I demonstrated by dipping both ends of a toothpick into the shallow cup filled with white glue. I laid the toothpick on the card and repeated the process for the other three toothpicks, reproducing Timmy's pattern on the construction paper.

"Does someone have a different arrangement?" I asked.

Elena volunteered. "My idea was to make a capital L," she said, and she rearranged the four toothpicks on the overhead projector.

"Who can explain why Elena's pattern fits the rules?" I asked.

Drew raised his hand and said, "They all touch, and there are two straight lines and one square corner."

I took another four toothpicks and built the reflection of Elena's "L" next to her pattern.

"What about this design?" I asked. "Is it different?"

Tanya spoke up. "It's the same," she said, "because if you flipped your shape, it would be the same as Elena's."

"I agree," chimed in Timmy and Gena.

"It's like the shapes we did with the triangles," Grant said. Others nodded.

We had discussed congruency before, but I knew that this was a good time to reinforce the concept. "Mathematicians say that when an arrangement is flipped or rotated to make exactly the same size and shape arrangement as another, the arrangements are congruent. They're not considered different patterns," I explained. "If you're not sure whether one of your patterns is congruent to another, it might help to draw your shape on a piece of newsprint and flip or rotate it to see if it's the same. If you hold your drawing up to a window, you can see what you drew when you flip it." I demonstrated by drawing the pattern I made and flipping it to show it was the same as Elena's "L."

I then arranged the four toothpicks on the overhead projector into a straight line as Timmy had, but I oriented it differently. I wanted to be sure students understood the test for congruency.

"What about this pattern?" I asked.

Alex responded. "If you turned it, it would be like Timmy's," he said, moving the four toothpicks on the overhead.

"I have another shape," Kendra said. She made a shape resembling the constellation the Big Dipper but with the bucket and handle meeting at right angles.

"Can someone make the same pattern Kendra made, but arrange it so that it looks different?" I asked. "Talk to your neighbor about an idea you think would work." The children began talking and gesturing.

"What do you think?" I asked after a few moments.

Mark said, "You could make this shape," and he proceeded to make what looked like a question mark without the dot.

I drew Mark's shape on a piece of paper and asked him to convince the class that it was the same as Kendra's. He smiled and held the paper up to the window, rotated it, and then flipped it to show it matched Kendra's Big Dipper.

"Mark's shape is congruent to Kendra's, so it's not a different shape," I said. "Your task is to find all the *different* arrangements possible with four toothpicks. What questions do you have?" There were none, so I asked the Group Supply People to collect the supplies.

### Observing the Children

"Mrs. Rectanus, George's hogging all the toothpicks and won't share," Felicia complained. I looked over at the table where George sat hunched, his arms protectively around the toothpick supply. Noticing that I was looking at him, George straightened up and said brightly, "See I'm sharing! Really!" He passed a handful of toothpicks to each of his group members.

"Well, he wasn't before," Felicia said, and she went back to the table.

The students worked for about 35 minutes. The room was noisy, but the noise was productive, as the children discussed the similarities and differences among their patterns. As I circulated throughout the room, observing the children and listening to their conversations, I heard comments such as: "No,

that's not a different one. You could just flip it and it'd be the same. Like this, see?" and "Look, this shape is a new one because the tail is different."

In many groups, the children seemed to delegate jobs naturally. Ben and Jenny created patterns and Gena and David glued them. Elena went from table to table, checking to see if other groups had found shapes her group hadn't. Every child was busy.

After about half an hour, five groups thought they had found all the possibilities. Confusion ensued, as students went to other tables to compare results. Finally, Kendra suggested that all groups that thought they were finished put their designs on the rug for everyone to see. I noticed that despite the hubbub, two groups remained working at their tables, apparently not distracted by the children on the rug.

Kendra took charge of the students on the rug. "Okay, everyone who found the straight line, put yours under ours." A column of five papers was created. She continued, "Okay, now the plus sign." She placed her group's paper next to the first one. The rest of the children followed suit. A fascinating color-coordinated rectangular array was developing.

"Now the square," instructed Emma, taking over from Kendra.

"Oh, we don't have that one," cried Maurice. "I'll make it!" He and Justin headed back to their table.

For about 10 more minutes, the children continued placing their patterns until they had created a 5-by-16 rectangular array. It filled most of the rug area, and students sat on desks or chairs to see all the arrangements. Children talked about whether shapes were congruent or not. Some groups found duplicates; others discovered patterns they had missed. Finally, the last two groups came over to add their results to the matrix.

"Do you think you've found them all?" I asked. "Yes!" was the overwhelming response.

Craig added, "It's like that problem we did with the four triangles. Since 31 heads all got the same answer, we must be right, because everyone knows that more heads together are smarter than 1 head alone!"

We left the cards on the rug for the glue to dry, and the children went outside for recess.

### A Class Discussion

When the children returned, I initiated a discussion about the activity. I was interested in the children's reaction to the problem. I posted Kendra's group's rectangles on the bulletin board. "What did you think of this activity?" I asked. The discussion focused on students' ideas about which patterns were easy to make and which were hard.

After about a half-dozen students had offered their ideas, Gordon raised his hand. "You're all going too fast," he complained. "I can't tell which shape you're talking about because just when I figure it out, someone moves on to another shape."

"What should we do about that?" I asked the class.

Several students had suggestions. Edward, Gordon's best friend, volunteered to help Gordon. Tanya said they should talk more slowly. Grant suggested holding up or pointing to the shape being discussed. Jenny said we should refer to each pattern by the letter it looked like. The class liked Jenny's idea best and decided to try it. This worked fine until Tom began talking about a design that didn't look like a letter.

"I'm confused again," Gordon said glumly.

"Why don't we label each card with a number," I suggested, "so when someone wants to talk about shape nine, for example, we'll all be able to identify it easily." The class thought this was a good idea.

I numbered the patterns posted on the board. Kendra's group had made all 16 of them, a feat that doesn't always happen in a class. However, the children's collaboration on the rug had been successful.

I directed the other groups to label their patterns with the same numbers as those on the posted patterns. I noticed that some children easily matched patterns by looking at the board and finding the identical pattern in their sets. Others, however, needed to go up to the board to check. I also told groups to make any patterns they were missing and let us know if they had any patterns that weren't posted. A few students suggested other patterns, but they all proved to be duplicates. It was the end of class, and I pinned Kendra's group's cards on the bulletin board for a class reference.

## Part 2: The Toothpick Game

The next day, I set out materials for each group. I made sure that extra sheets of dot paper and index cards were available. Also, I listed five directions on the board:

1. Copy the 16 patterns onto toothpick dot paper and number them.
2. Cut apart the dot paper patterns.
3. Cut four index cards into quarters.
4. Glue each dot paper pattern to a quarter of an index card.
5. Decorate the back of each card.

"Today you'll make a deck of playing cards to use in a game," I told the class. "With your group, you need to do five things."

I held up a sheet of dot paper and said, "This toothpick dot paper is ruled into 16 sections, one for each toothpick pattern. Copy each pattern in a separate section and label it with its number."

To model my directions, I copied pattern number 1 onto one of the dot paper sections and labeled it with the number 1. Then I drew and labeled pattern number 2.

"When you've drawn and numbered all 16 arrangements," I said, "cut them apart along the lines on the dot paper." I cut out the two patterns I had drawn.

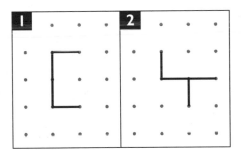

I continued, "Your group will also need to cut up four index cards to back the toothpick patterns for your deck of cards. The index card backs will make your dot paper designs easier to handle."

Taking a pair of scissors, I demonstrated how to cut the cards. "Fold a card in half lengthwise. Then open it up and fold it in half the other way. When you're done, your card should have two folds in it." Seven or eight children nodded.

"Cut the card along your fold lines to make four quarters," I said, cutting the first index card. "Then do the same for the other three cards."

Seeing a possibility to connect this lesson to the multiplication unit we had recently completed, I asked, "How many quarters will you have altogether when you're done?" "16," I heard about 10 students say.

"How do you know?" I wondered.

**NOTE** Children receive information in different ways. Some prefer to hear directions, some to read them, and others to be shown how to do something. One benefit of cooperative groups is a collective set of ears. At a given moment, not every child may be listening or understanding what is being presented; in groups, students can check with one another to clarify directions.

Nicole raised her hand. "Each card has four sections and there are four cards, and 4 times 4 is 16," she said.

"Raise your hand if you agree with Nicole's reasoning," I said. About 20 hands went up.

"Did someone figure it out a different way?" I asked.

Drew explained, "I thought there would be 8 pieces made from the first two cards, and 8 from the last two cards. 8 and 8 are 16, so there are 16 pieces," he finished.

"Do you agree with Drew's method?" I asked, and again, about 20 students raised their hands.

I continued, "Your group will need to do two more things. Glue each dot paper arrangement to a separate index card piece. Then create one design and use it to decorate the backs of the cards, so the backs of all your cards match."

"Can we make any design we want?" Craig wanted to know.

"As long as your group agrees," I answered. There were no further questions. Groups got their supplies and worked for the rest of the period. Kendra retrieved her group's patterns from the bulletin board, but I asked her to post them again after her group made its deck of cards.

## Introducing the Game

The next day I asked Julie, George, and David to demonstrate how to play a toothpick game with me, as the rest of the class sat in a semicircle around us on the rug.

"To play the toothpick game, your group needs its deck of toothpick cards and four toothpicks," I explained. "For a group of four, first choose any card and make the pattern with the toothpicks." I had George pick a card and build the pattern with toothpicks.

I continued, "Then shuffle that card back into the pack, and deal all the cards so each player has four. If you're a group of three, don't shuffle the beginning card back into the deck. Instead, leave it face up on the table. Then deal the remaining cards and you'll each have five."

"To play," I continued, "place your cards face up in front of you so everyone in your group can see them." Julie, George, David, and I placed our cards.

"The object of the game," I said, "is for all members of your group to be able to play all of their cards. Take turns. On your turn, you may play one card, as long as the pattern on that card can be made by changing the position of just one toothpick in the pattern on the table. Put the card next to the last one played and move one toothpick so the pattern of toothpicks matches the pattern on the card you played. The first player uses the toothpick pattern on the table as a guide." I stopped and put one of my cards next to the toothpick pattern on the rug. I had the students point out how they could make the pattern on my card by moving just one toothpick in the pattern on the rug. I moved the toothpick to make the pattern on my card.

"Help each other with moves and discuss the patterns," I said. "If everyone agrees with you that in a particular round you don't have a card you can play, you say, 'I pass.' If all the cards are played, your group has won. Sometimes though, you reach a point where no one can play another card. When you are stuck like that, you have to agree as a group that it's a stalemate."

**NOTE** Structuring the game so that children work together toward a common goal makes the emphasis of the game cooperative rather than competitive. Students benefit from many opportunities to work cooperatively.

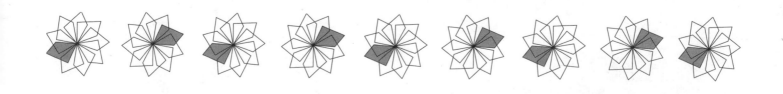

Julie, George, David, and I continued playing. Other students offered suggestions and help. We played all of our cards. The groups then played the game for the rest of the period. I circulated and watched them play.

About halfway through their game, Kendra, Courtney, and Gena stopped playing and tried to figure out which moves would help them win.

"If I play card 10, then Gena can change it into card 8," said Courtney excitedly. "Then, Kendra, you can change it into number 7, and I can change it to number 2."

"But then I can't play after that," Gena moaned in disappointment.

Courtney conceded, "Oh yeah, you're right."

The girls continued in this way, helping each other with moves until they found a way for their group to play all the cards. Then they actually played out the game to their satisfaction.

One group discovered they had lost a card, and Nichole offered to make a new one. She quickly cut out a new rectangle from the dot paper, and decorated an index card to match her group's deck. When she went to glue the design to the card, she realized that the index card was four times larger than her design. "Oops," she said, and glued the design to the card anyway, then cut the excess card away.

## A Class Discussion

Students played the game for the rest of the period and over the next week. At the end of that week, I initiated a class discussion about the game.

"How did you decide which card to play during each round?" I asked the children, who were gathered quietly on the rug.

There was a flurry of comments, and I waited for the class to become quiet once again. "Let's hear from one person at a time," I said. Several students raised their hands, and I called on Paul.

"I just asked Justin!" he said. The class giggled, and Justin said very quickly and enthusiastically, "Actually, I looked ahead to see where we would get stuck later. See, card 3, that's the square, and card 8, the straight line, were the hardest to work with because card 3 can only be made into 6, 11, 15, and 16, but card 8 can only turn into 7 and 10. So, if you get stuck with those two at the end, you're sunk! So we always tried to get rid of them first," he finished breathlessly. Some of the children began laughing because Justin had spoken so fast.

Edward spoke for many of the children when he said gently, "Boy, Justin, you said that too fast. Can you slow down a little?"

Justin looked somewhat embarrassed and replied, "Well, maybe someone else in our group should explain."

Sara spoke up. "What Justin's saying is that some of the cards are hard to use if you get stuck with them at the end of the game. Like the square. When we played, it was my last card. And Justin only had the straight line left. So when it was my turn, I put down my square, but then Justin couldn't play his straight line. So we lost." Several children nodded their agreement.

"What do you do when you get into a situation like that?" I asked.

David said, "Well, I try not to get into a situation like that in the first place!" The children laughed.

Kendra continued, "If you use the hard cards first, like the square and the straight line, then you have a better chance of winning. Gena and Courtney and I figured that out." I saw many students nod their head in agreement.

"Were other cards hard to play?" I asked. The children spontaneously began pointing to Kendra's group's posted cards and talking. I let them talk a bit before calling for attention. "One at a time, please," I said.

Maurice went first. He said, "The square and straight line could be hard to play, but really, what was hard depended on what you had to play with. So I think it's more if you can look ahead to see the trouble coming."

Gordon groaned, "That was the whole trouble with this game. I could never tell what was going to be hard or easy."

"But we helped you, Gordon," Timmy pointed out.

"Yeah, I guess so," Gordon conceded, "But I still didn't like the game very much. It was hard."

"I understand the difficulty some of you had with the game," I commented, "and I respect that maybe you didn't like playing it. Keep in mind that if you found it hard to see ahead to figure out what to play next, it may be that you need more experience moving shapes around in your head. This game and the other geometry activities we'll be doing will give you a lot of that kind of experience." I noticed that Gordon and some other children looked relieved.

### The Writing Assignment

"I'll need some help remembering what you've said today," I then said, "so please write about the strategies you used when you played the game. Include what you've discovered about patterns that are easy to change into others and those that are hard. Also, you might want to write about how your group worked together."

Timmy identified the easiest patterns to change and also talked about how his group worked.

> toothPick Game
>
> My Strategys are: the easyist thing to start is a four. I think the easyist to work with are —l because you can make l or 7 or 4 or ⅃ and you are likely to have it least one of these. I think are group worked ok but we fout some times because we could not agrey on the rouls. this game is fun because no buddy wins.

Elena wrote: *My strategy is to play the hard cards first so that I don't get stuck with them later in the game (Assuming the next person can go.) I think our group worked well because we weren't competing against each other. It's eaiser to help people than it is to compete against them.*

Gordon wrote: *This game was hard for me. I learned to work with a partner so if you got stuck they could help you.*

Cal wrote: *My stratigy is to always put the hardest ones to change down first. I learned to keep trying and to do the hardest cards to change. Like the line card can only change to two things. The F can change to lots of things.*

Gena wrote: *If you Do not get the ▢ or ---- that is good. Also if someone makes the ▢ or ---- and you Do not have to be the one to make another shape from the ▢ or ---- that is also good. I think that our group worked okay because we got silly some times and did't help the other people as much at the times we were silly. But the other times we hleped each other a lot.*

In her paper, Gena focused on two of the patterns.

> ## The ToothPick Game
>
> If you Do not get the ▢ or ─── that is good. Also if someone makes the ▢ or ─── and you Do not have to be the one to make another Shape from the ▢ or ─── that is also good. I think that our group worked Okay because we got Silly some times and did't help the other People as much at the times we were Silly. But the other times we hleped each other a lot.

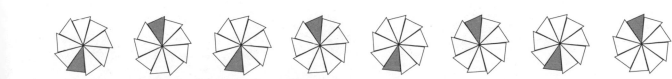

# WHOLE CLASS LESSON Investigating Boxes

## Overview

In this three-part lesson, students investigate three-dimensional shapes by examining boxes, comparing their similarities and differences, and sorting them by various properties. Students are introduced to standard mathematical language of polyhedra as they investigate the vertices, faces, and edges of the boxes. Also, by tracing the faces of their boxes, children gain experience relating two- and three-dimensional shapes.

In Part 1, children compare boxes and record the similarities and differences they notice. In Part 2, students sort the boxes into two groups by different attributes and then guess the ways others sorted their boxes. In Part 3, children trace the faces of a box.

The menu activity *Covering Boxes* (see page 104) extends the lesson by having children cover the faces and edges of their boxes with construction paper and yarn. The *Box Riddles* assessment (see page 111) has students write descriptions of their covered boxes, creating clues for others to use to match the riddles and boxes. The menu activity *Same and Different* (see page 62) is a related activity, a two-dimensional version of the comparing boxes activity in Part 1 of this lesson.

## Before the lesson

Gather these materials:
- 40–45 boxes of different sizes and shapes, including cylinders if possible (boxes should close or have lids)
- 15–20 sheets of 6-by-9-inch newsprint
- 15 sheets of 18-by-24-inch newsprint

## Teaching directions

For a week or two before the lesson, ask children to bring boxes to class. Tell them they should bring boxes with tops, either attached or separate. Supplement the supply so you have 10–12 more boxes than students.

### Part 1: Comparing Boxes

■ Explain to the children that they will work with a partner to compare boxes. Have each child choose a box and put it aside for later use.

■ Select two boxes from the remaining collection. Ask the class, "What do you notice about the boxes?" Have all students who are interested share their ideas. Also, introduce the geometric terminology of face, edge, and vertex, adding these words to the Geometry Words chart.

■ Have students discuss in pairs what is the same and different about the boxes they chose. They should record what they notice about both boxes. Observe children as they work. If you notice students focusing only on similarities or differences, offer suggestions to help them expand their thinking.

■ In a class discussion, ask pairs to read what they wrote. After each pair reports, ask the class for questions or suggestions.

## Part 2: Sorting Boxes

■ On another day, introduce the idea of sorting the boxes. To begin, choose six to eight boxes and sort them into two groups. For example, you can sort them into those with only rectangular faces and those with other shaped faces, or those that have attached tops and those that do not, or those that are cubes and those that are not. Ask the class to guess how you sorted the boxes. As you listen to the students, paraphrase their ideas, to model the use of correct geometric terminology.

■ Have children work in small groups of three or four. Each group needs six or seven boxes. Ask groups to sort their boxes into two sets in as many ways as they can, and to record how they did so.

■ After the children have recorded the ways they sorted their boxes, play a guessing game. Have groups choose one way they sorted their boxes and record each attribute they used on a 6-by-9-inch sheet of newsprint. Ask the rest of the class to guess how other groups sorted the boxes.

## Part 3: Tracing Faces

■ Before the lesson, choose one of the boxes you used for sorting and trace its faces onto a sheet of 18-by-24-inch newsprint. Show the children your tracings and ask them to guess which box you traced. Have them explain their reasoning.

■ Tell the children that each group will choose one box and trace all the faces as you did. Ask them for ideas about how to be sure they trace each face. Also, give the instruction that groups must trace all faces onto just one sheet of newsprint, unless they can prove to you that all the faces won't fit.

■ In a later class discussion, have groups describe how they accomplished the task.

## FROM THE CLASSROOM

### Part 1: Comparing Boxes

I gathered the class on the rug. "In this activity," I explained, "you and a partner each choose a box, then together examine both boxes. Your task is to notice what's the same and what's different about the boxes."

Immediately, Felicia raised her hand. "Can we use the box that we brought in?" she asked, referring to the four large shopping bags that held the boxes they had collected over the previous two weeks. Several students commented that they wanted to use their own boxes. Others looked anxiously at the bags.

I decided that until students had chosen their boxes, it would be difficult to hold their attention to explain the activity. "You can pick your box or a different one," I said. "Let's take the time for each of you to choose a box that you like. Put it on your desk and then come back to the rug."

A few minutes later, all the students were back on the rug, seemingly happy with their choices and better able to listen. I held up and slowly rotated two boxes for the class to see. One was a 5-by-5-by-12-inch box, a bit larger than a one-quart milk carton; the other was a 5-by-5-by-5-inch cube.

"What do you notice that's the same or different about the two boxes?" I asked. About 10 children raised their hands.

Elena began. "One's tall and thin and the other is short and sort of fat."

Alex continued. "And one is like a box that a bottle might come in, and the other . . . maybe it held a coffee mug."

Sara said, "They're not congruent to each other."

"Congruent?" I asked.

George blurted out, "The two boxes, if you put them next to each other they wouldn't match exactly because they're not the same. They just look sort of the same." Eight or nine students nodded their heads in agreement, including Sara.

"They both have six sides," Lisa said.

"What do you mean by sides?" I asked.

"You know, the sides are the pieces that hold the box together, and they have writing on them," Lisa replied, leaning over to touch one of the faces of the boxes.

"Mathematicians call those pieces 'faces,'" I said, taking the opportunity to introduce the correct mathematical vocabulary. "Let's check the number of faces on each box." The children counted along with me.

"What do you think these are called?" I pushed, running my finger along several edges of the boxes.

"Sides," several students called out.

"Edges!" said Tanya.

"Yes, they're called edges," I confirmed.

Gena, who doesn't often speak up in class, said softly, "I notice that each box has six faces, but they have . . . 11, no, 12 edges."

"That's twice as many edges as faces," said Edward.

I called on Paul. Paul could often be counted on during discussions to share his unique logic. "There's gotta be a special name for corners too, if sides are faces and where they meet are edges. Is there?" he asked.

"What do you think?" I asked the class.

Some children looked confused; others eagerly shouted yes; still others said maybe.

I continued, "As a matter of fact, Paul, there is a special name. Mathematicians call a corner a vertex. If they're talking about two or more corners, they say vertices—that's the plural. I'll add all these words to our Geometry Words chart so you can see how they're spelled."

Satisfied, Paul nodded, and slowly finished his original thought. "When we did the four-triangle problem, we learned that shapes with six sides and corners are hexagons, and shapes with eight sides and corners are octagons. But the boxes have six faces and eight corners." He demonstrated by counting the faces and edges on each box for the class to see. "What would you call that? A hexagon? An octagon?"

"What do you think?" I asked the class. "Talk to your neighbor about this." Paul's question sparked enthusiastic discussion among the children. I was fascinated by the children's interest and willingness to ponder it. After a minute or so, I asked the students for their attention.

"Who has an idea?" I asked.

Julie excitedly began, "Well, it doesn't make sense because Jenny and I agreed that a hexagon has six sides and six corners, and an octagon has eight sides and eight corners. So you can't really call it either because it fits both!" Several students who appreciated Julie's argument cheered.

"How about a hex-a-oct?" said Grant tentatively.

"Or oct-hex?" said Mark.

"Actually, mathematicians have several different names they use for boxes like this," I said, holding up one of the boxes. "It's called a polyhedron, and it can also be called a rectangular prism. I'll write these words on our chart."

I then gave the children instructions. "With a partner," I said, "look at your two boxes. Talk about what's the same about your boxes and what's different. Record all that you notice." The students found partners and began to work. I took this opportunity to add "faces," "edges," "vertex," and "vertices," "polyhedron," and "rectangular prism" to the Geometry Words chart.

### Observing the Children

I listened to the children's conversations and observed them working. The students were engaged and interested in the activity. I noticed that many of them ruled their papers into two columns, one for "Same" and one for "Different," while others just listed their observations.

As they worked, several pairs of students asked for my help. Some felt stuck for ideas, and others needed help describing a particular attribute. I also intervened with a few pairs who were having difficulty working together, either disagreeing about how to record or who was to record.

After about 20 minutes, all of the children had recorded at least a few similarities and differences. I waited a few minutes more and decided to call for the children's attention. It seemed that most of the students had run out of ideas, and some conversations had turned to social interests instead of mathematics.

**NOTE** Teachers must decide when to offer a recording structure and when to allow students to decide for themselves how to present their work. Either way, the assignment should provide children with the challenge of expressing their ideas in their own words.

Grant and Ben organized their paper as Emma and Tanya did.

Same and Different

They both have 6 faces.

1 G's box is smaller than B's box.

2 They both open the same way.

2 G's box fits inside B's box, but B's box doesn't fit in G's box.

3 They both have 8 corners.

4 They both have 12 edges

3 B's says Deluxe on it and G's says Macy's.

4. B's box has designs on it and G's box is plain.

5 They are both rectangels

6 They both open from the top.

7 They both have 2 pieces

Emma and Tanya organized their paper into two columns. Emma recorded in the "Same" column, and Tanya wrote in the "Different" column.

## SAME and DIFFERENT

**SAME**

① Both have 6 faces.
② Both have 12 edges.
③ Both have 8 corners.
④ Both are boxes.
⑤ Both have rips.
⑥ They both can be taken apart.
⑦ They both open-up.
⑧ They both have 2 triangles, and 2 trapizoids shapes on the bottom.

**DIFFERENT**

① Ones white and gray and ones maroon.
② Ones a rectangle, and ones a square.
③ One has writing and the other does not.
④ One is taller than the other.
⑤ One opens like a shoe box and one like a clam.
⑥ One has numbers the other does not.
⑦ One is recycleble.
⑧ One has tape.

### A Class Discussion

To begin the class discussion, I explained the procedure we would use to share our findings. My goal was for students to listen to and think about one another's ideas. "Each pair will report three or four things you found. Use your boxes to show us what you mean," I said. "Take a few moments to decide how you will make your presentation."

I called on Emma and Tanya first. *"Both have 12 edges,"* Emma read, while Tanya counted the edges for the class. *"Both have 8 corners,"* Emma continued, and again, Tanya counted.

"So did ours!" Grant called out, and his partner, Ben, nodded his agreement.

Emma continued reading while Tanya demonstrated. *"Both have rips. Ones a rectangle, and ones a square."*

"What do you mean?" asked Craig.

Tanya responded, "Well, my box looks like a square, and Emma's looks like a rectangle."

I took this opportunity to reinforce the use of correct mathematical language. "Mathematicians call both of your boxes rectangular prisms," I said, "but one is also a called a cube." I got up and wrote "cube" on the Geometry Words chart.

Grant and Ben went next. Grant read while Ben held the boxes. *"They are both rectangels."*

I interrupted. "The official name is rectangular prism," I said.

"Oh, yeah," Grant said.

"Let's all say 'rectangular prism,'" I said, and we all said it together.

**NOTE** It's valuable to provide the correct terminology whenever possible. From hearing words in the contexts of first-hand experiences, children can become familiar and comfortable with them.

Grant then continued reading: *"Grant's box fits inside Ben's box, but Ben's box doesn't fit in Grant's box. They both open the same way. They both open from the top."*

David and Gena reported next. David read shyly, while Gena showed their boxes: *"They are from different store's. You can smuash both of them. They both have 16 teen corrner's."*

Gena and David listed their discoveries, marking each with "S" or "D" to indicate when they were the same or different.

> D. One is gray and one is red.
> S. you can smuash Both oP Them
> S They Both have a stores name on them.
> D. One has a clear top and the They Doesnt.
> S. They both have 16 teen cornner's.
> S. They are Both Boxes.
> S. they Both Have 20 faces.
> D. One is bigger than the other.
> S. They Both are rectangals.
> D They are from Different stores.

Next Kendra read while Noah held the boxes: *"There both made of cardboard. Thae both feel the same inside. ones bumpy ones smooth. Thae bothe create static if you rub it on your head."*

The reporting continued in this way until it was time for lunch. Students had noticed many things about their boxes and enjoyed sharing them with the class. The variety of ideas shared, the range of language, and the students' enthusiasm for the activity made the discussion an exciting way to end math that day.

Kendra and Noah first wrote about how their boxes were the same and then about how they were different.

> same
> There both boxes.
> There both white insid.
> There both made of cardboard
> Thae both feel the same inside.
> Thae both create static if you rub it on your head.
> Different
> There dieint shaPes.
> ones bback ones white.
> Ones small Ones big.
> ones got writing ones doesnt.
> ones bumpy ones smooth.
> ones got a lid that can came off
> ones got a flap lid.

## Part 2: Sorting the Boxes

We continued with the boxes activity the next day. For the benefit of the two children who were absent the day before, I began class by asking the children to review what we had done. Then I introduced the idea of sorting the boxes. To prepare for this, I had chosen seven boxes and sorted them into two groups—those with all rectangular faces and those with other shaped faces. In one group, I put five boxes with rectangular faces—a shoe box, a shirt box, and boxes that had held a tie, thank-you cards, and tissues. Into the other group I put a cylindrical oatmeal box and a hexagonal tube that had held fireplace matches.

"How do you think I chose to sort these boxes?" I asked. The students began to talk with one another. After a few minutes, I called for their attention. "I'd like to hear all of your ideas," I said.

Courtney began, pointing to the cylinder. "Those have circles or funny shapes and those are regular boxes?"

Rather than respond to Courtney's idea, I asked, "Does anyone have a different idea?"

Noah guessed next. "The faces of all those are rectangles and the others aren't," he said.

I called on Kendra. "Those five all have 12 edges and the other two are boxes that have . . . well, they don't have 12 edges," she confidently said.

George waved his hand back and forth. "I know!" he boomed. "Those five have square corners and the other two don't!"

Lisa continued. "Some held gifts and some didn't," she said.

"I'm going to show how you can record your ideas," I said, moving to the overhead projector. "Courtney's idea could be written as 'has circular faces' and 'doesn't have circular faces.' Noah's idea could be written as 'has rectangular faces' and 'doesn't have rectangular faces,'" I recorded these ideas on the overhead.

"For Kendra's idea," I said as I continued recording, "I could write 'has 12 edges' and 'doesn't have 12 edges.' What about George's idea?"

"Square corners and no square corners," George said. I recorded his suggestion.

I then explained to the students that each table group should add two more boxes to its collection so that each group had six boxes to sort. The group was then to sort the boxes in as many different ways as possible, recording all the ways, as I had done on the overhead.

### Observing the Children

The students were busy at work as I circulated among the groups, answering questions and listening to the children's ideas.

George, Felicia, Paul, and Mark were supposed to work together since they sat at the same table, but Paul had left to go to an appointment and Mark was absent. George and Felicia decided not to work with anyone else. In retrospect, I wish I had asked them to work with another small group of three children. The two argued over which boxes to add to make a collection of six, how to sort the boxes, and who had to record. I found myself spending more time than I would have liked trying to help these two children solve their problems.

When it seemed as if George and Felicia had finally found a way to share their thinking and the work, I left them, only to find out later that they had compared only their two individual boxes and ignored the rest. They recorded their results as they had in Part 1 of the lesson: *Same: My box has six sides and so dose hers. They ech have sides. Different: Felicia's box is shiney. george's box is dull. Georges has 12 and I have 28.* [I didn't know what they were referring to here.] *I have flaps and she does not.*

Later I talked with George and Felicia to determine if they had misunderstood the assignment. Felicia said, "I know. We were supposed to write things like . . . like 'has six sides' and 'doesn't have six sides.' I guess we just got carried away and forgot."

The other groups recorded a variety of ways to sort the boxes. For example, Cal, Nicole, and Gena wrote: *1. boxes with big letters on them and the others that don't. 2. square corners and not. 3. Those that are roughd and those that arn't. 4. same shape and not same shape. 5. boxes with six faces and boxes without six faces. 6. boxs from a deparment store and those that arn't.*

Sara, Emma, and Drew listed 17 ways to sort their boxes, focusing on texture, color, number of faces, shapes of the faces, and more.

Sara, Emma, and Drew found 17 ways to sort their boxes.

1. Food and not food
2. Pictures and no Pictures.
3. 6 faces and not 6 faces.
4. Plastic tops and not Plastic tops.
5. Cylinders and not Cylinders.
6. Silver and no silver.
7. Words and no words.
8. Circle top and rectangle top.
9. #s and no #s.
10. Unfold and not unfold.
11. Aluminum and not Aluminum.
12. Rips and no rips.
13. Activities and no Activities.
14. Smooth and rough.
15. Creases and no creases.
16. Gold and no gold.
17. Stickers and no stickers

Courtney, Elena, and Craig included how many boxes belonged in each set.

1. 3 Are used for carrying food and 3 arent.
2. 5 Are card bord one is tin.
3. 5 Are Rectangle's one is a cube.
4. 2 Have Gold and 4 don't.
5. They all have white in them or on them
6. One steel has Ceral the rest do not.
7. they all have six faces.
8. 4 you can take off there lids and two you can't.
9. 5 have words on them and 1 does not.
10. 2 have silver and 4 don't.
11. 4 have strip's and 2 don't
12. One is all white and five don't
12. 2 Carly Candy and 4 don't
13. one has people on it.

### A Class Discussion

Before class the next day, I took two sheets of 6-by-9-inch newsprint and wrote "All Rectangular Faces" on one and "Not All Rectangular Faces" on the other. I placed the seven boxes I had used in the previous day's lesson into two groups, one on either side of me on a bookshelf, then posted the correct description over each group. I turned the newsprint labels over, however, so the children couldn't read what I had written.

"I've sorted the boxes we used yesterday and written how I sorted them on the other side of these papers," I told the class, seated on the rug around me. "What do you think I've written on them? Talk to your neighbor."

Gordon offered his idea first. "Lids that come off and lids that don't," he said.

"Boxes with blue on them and boxes without," Julie contributed.

"Keep guessing," I said. "Your answers show that a lot of ideas work. Let's see how many ways you can think of before I show you what I wrote."

Emma said, "Boxes with square corners and boxes without."

"Rectangular faces and not rectangular faces," Craig offered.

Justin pointed out, "But the box with the hexagons has some rectangles." Craig shrugged.

Kendra raised her hand. "Like I said yesterday, 12 edges or not 12 edges."

After everyone who wanted to contribute an idea had done so, I turned over the papers. I deliberately hadn't turned them over when Craig guessed correctly. I wanted to encourage the children to pursue their thinking.

I then told the children, "Your group is to choose one of the ways you sorted your boxes yesterday. Record the attributes on two sheets of newsprint, as I did. Then we'll come back to the rug and try to guess how each group sorted its boxes." Although some groups initially had trouble agreeing on which attribute to choose, after about five minutes the students had returned to the rug.

**NOTE** Giving answers often results in stopping students' thinking. Children need to learn to be persistent, even when an answer is not immediately obvious. When teachers don't tell answers, students get the message that it's important for them to continue thinking about a problem until they make sense of it.

I explained what we would do. "When it's your group's turn, bring your boxes to the bookshelf and sort them. Pin the label sheets above the boxes, with the writing facing the wall. Then the class will guess how you sorted the boxes. When someone guesses, either say that the guess was correct and show the cards or ask the person to try again. You can tell students if they're close, but ask them to explain a different way."

I asked Noah, Paul, and Kendra to begin. They put a small, white hexagonal-shaped box on one side of the bookshelf, and four rectangular-faced boxes and one cylinder on the other side.

Courtney began the guessing. "That one is small and those aren't?"

"Nope," said Noah.

Courtney tried again. "One's a hexagon and those aren't?"

"No," Noah said again.

Paul called on Maurice, who said, "The single box has 12 edges and the others don't."

Kendra replied, "No."

Craig guessed next. "The white box doesn't have words on it and the others do."

Kendra looked carefully at the boxes and smiled. "That's true," she said, "but it's not how we sorted them."

Justin offered, "The single box has more faces?"

Noah shook his head.

The class was stymied. Then Courtney spoke up again, saying, "The single box can fit triangles in it and the others can't." I was interested in how Courtney knew this, but I didn't interrupt.

Kendra shook her head. "Not it," she responded. "Do you need a hint?"

"YES!" the class shouted. Kendra, Paul, and Noah put their heads together and whispered. Then Paul said, "One word starts with an S."

Courtney tried again. "The single box has 18 edges?"

Justin replied, "That doesn't start with an S, Courtney."

"She's right," Noah said, "but it's not how we sorted them."

"It had earrings in it?" Courtney asked.

"Close," said Paul.

The guesses came fast and furiously.

"Jewelry?" offered Elena.

"Something to wear?" from Justin.

"Gold?" asked George.

"Silver?"

"No, no, no!" Kendra, Noah, and Paul replied. They were laughing at the determined guessing. "Do you need another hint?"

"Yes!" cried the class again.

Finally the group said, "It has nothing to do with faces, edges, or corners."

A few minutes later, the class still hadn't guessed. I finally asked, "Is there any way for us to guess from just looking at the boxes?"

"Well . . . ," Noah replied, "not really. It's heck of hard!"

It was time for lunch, so we decided to leave the boxes where they were and try again later.

After lunch, Courtney burst into the classroom. "Kendra told me at recess how they sorted the boxes," she cried. "There's no way we can figure it out! You absolutely cannot tell from looking at them."

**NOTE** Children often think and work in ways teachers may not expect, so teachers should always be interested in and curious about students' ideas. It's important not to look for specific responses but to be open to new directions.

**NOTE** It's important to ask children to explain their answers. Requiring children to elaborate on their answers helps reveal their reasoning processes and gives them the message that their thinking, not just their answers, is important.

Kendra grinned sheepishly. "Well . . . I guess you're right. Do you want to know or want to keep guessing?" she asked the class, who had settled down on the rug.

"Tell!" most of the class replied.

Paul turned over the label cards. On them were written, "Had something in them," and "Didn't have anything in it."

This was not what I had expected. Yet it was a good reminder to me that children do things in ways adults may not expect.

We continued the group sharing over the next few days. Attributes students came up with were: boxes with gold print on them and those without, six faces and not six faces, boxes made in the U.S. and boxes made elsewhere, and circular faces and no circular faces.

## Part 3: Tracing Faces

I showed the class a piece of 18-by-24-inch drawing paper on which I had traced the six faces of the shirt box I used when I sorted boxes. "I've traced all the faces of one of the boxes I sorted the other day," I explained. "I wonder if you can tell from the tracing which box I used. Talk to your neighbor about it." There was an immediate murmur of conversation and much pointing at the boxes.

"Does anyone have an idea to share?" I asked. I called on Julie.

"I think you traced this one," she said, coming up to pick up the shirt box. More than half the class nodded in agreement.

"How do you know?" I asked, wanting to hear her explanation.

Holding the box against my drawing, Julie said, "I knew it couldn't be the tissue box because it's a lot smaller than the big rectangle. I knew it couldn't be the oatmeal can because . . ." she faltered momentarily, searching for words to express her thought. "Because you didn't draw a circle. I also knew it couldn't be the hexagon poster box because then the rectangles would be long and skinny and probably wouldn't fit on the paper."

Craig raised his hand and said, "It couldn't be the tie box because the tie box is long and skinny. The thank-you cards are too small; that's obvious. So it had to be the shirt box."

"How could you find out for sure?" I asked.

"Hold the box up to your paper and see," said Justin, exasperated. "Like Craig said, it's obvious." He took the shirt box from Jessie and held it against my paper, rotating it so that everyone could see that the faces of the box match my drawings.

"I'm curious about what my tracing will look like if I trace the cylinder," I said, as I held up the oatmeal box. "What do you think? Discuss your ideas with someone sitting nearby."

After a few minutes I asked, "Is anyone willing to venture a guess?"

Edward volunteered, "I think you'll get two small circles for the ends and one big circle for the middle."

Jenny raised her hand. "I think you'll get two small circles, but I don't think you'll get a big circle. I think you'll get a rectangle instead."

"Huh?" replied Edward.

"Look," said Jenny, "imagine you cut the oatmeal box straight down the side and lay it flat. You'd get a rectangle, not a circle."

NOTE Teachers need not always resolve questions, even when children are confused. It's best for children to resolve confusion for themselves, rather than merely hear the right answer in a class discussion.

Edward looked at Jenny dubiously. Other children looked confused. I decided not to resolve the children's confusion and instead discuss it again after they had finished the activity.

"With your group," I instructed, "choose one of your boxes and trace the faces onto a sheet of 18-by-24-inch newsprint." I showed them the paper they were to use.

"Make sure that you trace each face," I continued. "How can you be sure you've done that?"

Grant quickly said, "You could write a number on each face and then once you've traced it, write the same number on the paper."

"Does someone have a different idea?" I asked.

"You could use letters instead of numbers," Tanya offered.

"Or mark each face with your pencil after you trace it," Ben suggested.

"One last instruction," I told the children. "Make sure you can fit your faces onto one sheet of paper. If you think you need another sheet, you'll have to prove to me first that all the faces of your box won't fit on one sheet."

### Observing the Children

The children eagerly got to work. They seemed to enjoy the tracing and cooperated well with one another. Some children traced, some measured, some cut out the pieces, and others held a box while someone else traced around it.

"I can't believe they all fit on one piece of paper!" was one comment I heard frequently, as well as "Look! This shape is exactly the same as that shape!"

Most groups chose to trace their faces onto the paper without first planning how to arrange them. Justin and his group, however, measured the dimensions of their box and cut out templates. Then they arranged and rearranged the templates on their paper until they found a way to fit all of the faces of their box on one sheet of paper.

### A Class Discussion

In a class discussion, all the groups had a chance to explain how they had accomplished the task. Several groups reported how they had saved space by tracing faces next to one another. Edward commented that his group had thought that the paper wouldn't be big enough for all the shapes. "But it was," he said, "because we were careful." Justin explained his group's system for making templates for all the faces; other students seemed impressed with this method.

Two groups had traced cylindrical boxes and were eager to explain their methods to the others. Emma spoke for her group. "We chose the oatmeal box because it looked . . . weird. Anyway, I made a little line starting at the top and going down the side of the can about an inch. Then we laid the box on our paper and Jessie got down close to the desk top to see if the line was right on the paper. When we got it right, we traced along the lid as we rolled the box until the line got back to where it started from." Some of the children were in awe; others looked confused.

"How did you end up with a rectangle?" Paul wanted to know.

Emma answered, "I just *knew* it would be a rectangle. I closed my eyes and imagined what it would look like."

Kendra interrupted and said, "Our group had the potato chip can and we didn't know what shape we were going to get. So Alex decided to cut the can open, and we got a rectangle. See?" Kendra held up the drawing while Alex showed the cut-open can to the class.

Julie added, "I'm with you, Kendra and Alex. I didn't know what we'd get either, even though Emma said it'd be a rectangle. I guess I had to see it to believe it!"

I knew that Emma loved to sew and draw and that she was quite competent at both for a third grader. The children's conversation reminded me that the development of spatial visualization requires a variety of experiences over time with two-dimensional and three-dimensional objects.

# CONTENTS

# MENU ACTIVITIES

The activities on the menu were selected to offer children a variety of ways to think about geometric ideas. The menu was constructed with the consideration that not all children engage with or experience concepts in the same way; it includes activities that appeal to different interests and aptitudes.

The menu serves several purposes. First of all, the menu activities offer children ways to extend their experiences with whole class lessons. *Same and Different, Rotating Designs,* and *Four-Triangle Color Arrangements* extend *The Four Triangle Problem* lesson. The *Put-in-Order Problem* extends the *Toothpick Patterns* lesson. *Square Up* is a game that does not extend a specific lesson, but gives children additional practice with spatial visualization and strategic thinking. *Covering Boxes* extends the *Investigating Boxes* lesson.

The menu also solves the classroom problem of students who finish activities more quickly than others. For example, in Part 3 of the whole class lesson *Investigating Boxes,* as the children finish tracing the faces of their boxes, they can choose a menu activity. In this way, they stay meaningfully engaged with the mathematics of the unit even though they have completed the requirement for the whole class lesson.

In addition, the menu benefits students by providing a structure for independent learning. Once students are familiar with several menu activities, they can work on different activities during the same math period and can work at their own pace. In this way, the menu gives students control over their learning and helps them learn to make choices and manage their time.

The menu also benefits teachers. When children are working independently, the teacher doesn't have the major responsibility for leading a lesson. Instead, he or she can work with individuals, pairs, or small groups and initiate discussions that give valuable insights into students' thinking, reasoning, and understanding.

### The Importance of Class Discussions

While the menu activities provide children experience with geometric ideas, class discussions are essential for cementing and furthering student learning. Class discussions help students express their ideas, hear the ideas of others, and develop and strengthen their understanding. These discussions also provide teachers with opportunities to receive feedback about activities and assess what students have learned.

A class discussion is most beneficial after students have had time to interact with a menu activity and engage with the geometric ideas. The "From the Classroom" section for each menu activity contains valuable suggestions for leading class discussions. The situations described in these sections will not be the same in other classrooms, but they are representative of what typically occurs, and the teacher's responses are useful models for working with students during menu time.

### Classroom Suggestions

The "Notes About Classroom Organization" section on page 6 provides information about organizing the classroom for menus. Following are additional suggestions.

Because the menu activities relate to previous instruction in whole class lessons, students are somewhat prepared for them. However, menu activities need to be introduced carefully so that children understand what you are asking them to do. When children are clear about what is expected of them, they're more able to function as independent learners. Specific teaching directions are provided in the "Getting Started" section of each menu activity.

Also, it's best to introduce activities just one or two at a time during the unit. The suggested daily schedule on pages 8–11 offers one plan for introducing menu activities and structuring menu time for the unit.

Giving clear directions is not sufficient for helping children learn to work independently. Additional time and attention are required. For example, menu activities that require students to work in pairs are marked with a "P" in the upper right-hand corner; those that can be done individually are marked with an "I." Children might need to be reminded from time to time that information about a menu activity is available to them on the written menu tasks. Also, you might need to review directions several times on several different days to be sure that children understand and remember what to do.

### Providing Ongoing Support

You may find it useful at times to offer children models for an activity. For example, *Same and Different* asks children to compare polygons and write about how they are different. After some children have completed this assignment, you might invite a few pairs who have successfully completed the work to read their papers to the class. Examples of acceptable work can help others who haven't yet completed the assignment. Be careful, however, to choose only work that offers positive models so that no child's work is used as a negative example.

At other times, before having the children begin work on menu activities, you might want to have a discussion about working with partners. Have

the children talk about how they are helpful to each other. Ask them to bring up problems they've encountered and either describe how they resolved them or ask the class for suggestions. You may want to report what you've observed about children working independently and cooperatively. These discussions are invaluable for helping students learn to be productive learners.

Although students are encouraged to make choices and pursue activities of interest to them during menu time, they also should be required to try all of the menu activities. Be aware, however, that children will respond differently to activities. Not all children get the same value out of the same experiences; students will engage fully with some activities and superficially with others. This is to be expected and respected. Also, each activity can be revisited several times, and the menu gives children the opportunity to return to those activities that especially interest them.

## MENU ACTIVITY

# Same and Different

### Overview

*Same and Different* extends students' experiences in the whole class lesson *The Four-Triangle Problem.* (See page 16.)

In this activity, students use the polygons created during that lesson to compare and contrast figures. Children each choose a four-triangle shape and work in pairs to compare and contrast the attributes of the two shapes. They describe in writing how the polygons are the same and how they are different. Note: This comparing activity is a two-dimensional version of the comparing boxes activity in Part 1 of the whole class lesson *Investigating Boxes.* (See page 46.)

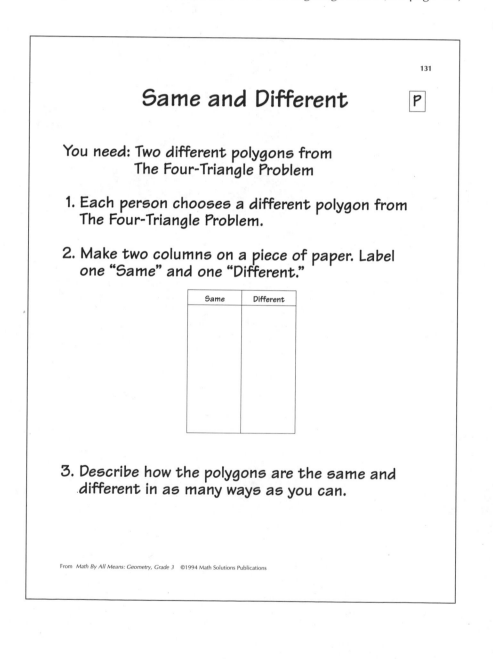

131

## Same and Different   P

You need: Two different polygons from
The Four-Triangle Problem

1. Each person chooses a different polygon from The Four-Triangle Problem.

2. Make two columns on a piece of paper. Label one "Same" and one "Different."

| Same | Different |
|------|-----------|
|      |           |

3. Describe how the polygons are the same and different in as many ways as you can.

## Before the lesson

Gather these materials:
- Sets of four-triangle polygons the students made in the whole class lesson *The Four-Triangle Problem* (See page 16.)
- Tape or glue
- One stapler
- Blackline master of menu activity, page 131

## Getting started

■ Choose two polygon shapes from *The Four-Triangle Problem* and show them to the class. Ask: "How are these two shapes alike or different?" Have students describe what they notice.

As students begin to offer their ideas, demonstrate how to organize information for recording. Make two columns on the board and label one "Same" and the other "Different." Record the children's statements in the appropriate columns.

■ Tell the students that they will work in pairs and choose two polygons. Together they will look for similarities and differences in the two shapes. Then they will record their findings.

■ Over several days, have children present to the class their comparisons of the polygons they chose. Encourage students to listen to one another's ideas and, if they'd like, suggest additions. Have children post their papers and the shapes they used.

**NOTE** Students' presentations during class discussions provide opportunities for informal assessment of their understanding of geometric ideas and vocabulary. Written work provides additional insights.

## FROM THE CLASSROOM

I ruled two columns on the overhead projector and labeled one "Same" and one "Different." I held up two shapes from the Polygon graph—the square and one of the parallelograms. I asked, "What do you notice about these two polygons?"

Kendra began, "I see squares in both. The parallelogram is made with a square in the middle and the square is . . . one whole square."

"Where should I record Kendra's statement?" I asked, pointing to the columns I had labeled.

"Under 'Different,'" George blurted out. I wrote:

> The parallelogram is made with a square in the middle, and the square is one whole square.

"What else do you notice?" I asked.

Nicole said, "The square has two blue triangles touching each other, and the parallelogram doesn't. Write that under 'Different.'"

Gena spoke next. "I have a 'Same' one: Both shapes can be made from four triangles," she said. I recorded her suggestion in the "Same" column.

"Look, the square doesn't have points the way the parallelogram does!" Elena offered excitedly.

Kendra joined the conversation again. "What she means," Kendra said, "is that the points on the parallelogram are more pointy than the square."

"Does anyone know what we call the points?" I asked the class.

"Corners?" Lisa offered.

"Angles?" said Jenny.

"Mathematicians call the points vertices," I said, "and the line segments that come together to make a vertex form an angle." I traced several angles by running my finger along several pairs of sides. "Angles are different sizes. The pointy angles are smaller and the wider ones are larger." I stopped to write "angles" on the class Geometry Words chart.

"What should I write about Elena's observation?" I then asked.

Elena said, "Both have angles. Write it under 'Same.'"

Gordon and David compared the parallelogram and one of the hexagons. They wrote about symmetry in both columns.

> # Same and Different
>
> **Same**
> ① They have 4 triangles.
> ② They are both shapes.
> ③ They Both Dont have symmetry
> ④ You can think of them as different shapes
> Ⓝ They Both have corners and sides.
>
> **Different**
> ① One has 4 sides and One has 6 sides.
> ② One is Longer they other.
> ③ They Both Do Not have symmetry
> ④ One has 4 Sides and one doesnt
> ⑤ One is a Quadri Laeral and one is a Hexogon.

Grant volunteered next. "I notice that both shapes have parallel lines," he remarked. He came up and traced the parallel sides of the square and the parallelogram to show what he meant.

"Parallel lines?" Cal asked.

"Sure, they're lines that are the same distance from each other and go on forever and ever without touching. Like railroad tracks," Grant said.

"But railroad tracks don't go on forever," Cal countered.

At a loss, Grant looked at me for help, but then he said to Cal, "I know railroad tracks don't go on forever. Maybe I should have said that *if* the tracks went on forever, they'd never meet."

"But I've seen where two tracks come together, like when a train has to go from one track to another," remarked Justin.

"Okay, okay," said Grant, frustrated, "I don't mean that railroad tracks never meet, but that lots of times the tracks are parallel."

I wasn't surprised by the dialogue the boys were having. Grant is a highly verbal child whose parents spend a great deal of time explaining things to him using adult language. He loves to read and has a strong and vivid imagination. At the same time, Cal isn't afraid to ask questions during class discussions, and his questions often lead the class in interesting directions.

"You're right Grant," said Cal. "Let's write 'They both have parallel lines.'"

I recorded Cal's idea and then added "parallel" to the Geometry Words chart. I pointed out that "parallel" was part of the word "parallelogram" that was already on the chart.

After several more students offered suggestions, I told the class, "For this activity, your job is to find a partner and choose two different shapes from the ones you made in *The Four-Triangle Problem*. Look carefully at the shapes and describe to each other what you notice is the same and what is different about the two shapes. Record your sentences when you both agree on what to write." There were no questions, and the class began menu work.

### A Class Discussion

A few days later, I brought the class together so that children could share their discoveries. I knew that some of them hadn't completed or even started the activity, but I felt that hearing other students' ideas would be helpful.

Courtney and Gena came up to share first. They had chosen to compare the square and the triangle.

Courtney read what they had written in the "Same" column: *"They are both made out of 4 triangles. There both shapes. They both have purple on them. they are both made out of tagbord. they both have tan on them."*

Courtney passed the paper to Gena, who read what they had recorded in the "Different" column: *"One is a square and one is a triangle. The square donest'n have a square in it. The square is made out of 2 triangle's and the triangle is made out of 1. The triangle looks like the top of a rocket ship and the square dose not. The square has 4 corners and the triangle has 3."*

The class paid close attention to the girls. "Wow," Tom commented. "They wrote a lot." The girls looked pleased.

"Maybe some of Courtney and Gena's discoveries give you some ideas for your shapes," I said. I wanted the children to know that it was fine to learn from one another's ideas.

Emma and Grant reported next. They had found many things that were the same about the two hexagons that the children thought looked like rocketships.

Emma read their entries in the "Same" column: *"1. They both have a blue triangle sticking up like a rocket ship. 2. They both have a gap at the bottom shaped like a triangle. 3. They both have two blue triangles. 4. They both have two green triangles. 5. They both have triangles stiking out at the bottom but in a diffritn way. 6. They both have 6 sides."* She then read the three things that they had written were different about their polygons: *"1. One shape is wider than the other. 2. The thin one has a square in it and the fat one dosen't. 3. the thin one has a green triangle the wide one does not."* Grant pointed out to the class the picture they had drawn and colored to help explain their last statement.

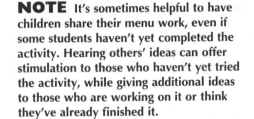

Emma and Grant wrote about the two hexagons that looked like rocket ships.

> **Same** | **Differnt**
>
> **Same**
> 1 They both have a blue triangle sticking up like a rocketship.
> 2. They both have a gap at the bottom shaped like a triangle.
> 3. They both have two blue triangles.
> 4. They both have two green triangles.
> 5. They both have triangles sticking out at the bottom but in a diffrnt way.
> 6. They both have 6 sides.
>
> **Differnt**
> 1. One shape is wider than the other.
> 2. The thin one has a square in it and the fat one dosen't.
> 3. the thin one has a green triangle and the wide one does not.

Craig and Ben volunteered to read next. They had compared the rectangle and one of the pentagons.

Their recording reminded me that students are often more capable than we realize. Craig read first: *"Same: They are Both 2-D. They Both have Big triangles in them. Half of Ben's shape shown in fig. 1. (dotted line means fold) Equaals to the long side of Craigs shape."* The boys had made a sketch to illustrate their point and Craig pointed this out to the class. I was surprised to see their use of the phrase "fig. 1."

Then Ben read from the "Different" column: *"Different: Ben's is a pentagon and Craig's is a quadrilateral. Ben's has 5 points, and Craig's has 4. Craig's is 6" by 3," and Ben's is 9" by 4" by 3" by 4" by 3"."*

No other children volunteered to read. "I'll post the three papers you heard, so others can look at them for ideas," I said. "I think it would be a good idea to have the shapes you compared posted next to your writing, so tape them to another sheet and put your names on it." The children nodded.

As other children completed their work, I posted their work. From time to time over the next few weeks, children read and added ideas to the papers they had already posted on the bulletin board, or made suggestions to their classmates about things they might add. The work proved to be a rich source for discussion throughout the unit.

Eventually, we moved the work to the bulletin board in the hall and invited other classes to examine the comparisons and add their ideas about what was the same and what was different about the pairs of polygons.

Jenny and Julie chose two hexagons.

Same and Different

| Same | Different |
|------|-----------|
| ① they Both have two Blues and two Greens. | ① Is biger then the other. |
| ② They both have Six Sides. | ② One look's like a bird and the other look's like the sate of Calisornia. |
| ③ They are both Shapes. | |
| ④ They both have squares made inside them. | ⑤ One is longer then the other. |
| ⑤ they both have triangles inside them. | |

Tom and Drew compared the trapezoid and one of the hexagons. They erroneously stated that both were parallelograms, instead of that both had parallelograms inside them.

Same and Different

| Same | Different |
|------|-----------|
| Both have 4 triangles. | One is a △△ and the other is a ▷. |
| They both have 2 blue and a green Triangles. | There both ararge in a different patern. One has a triangle made in it and the other does not. |
| They are both Parallelgorams. | The △△ has 4 and the other has 6. |
| They both have a □ made in it. | One has a big triangle in it and the other doesn't. |

# MENU ACTIVITY

# Rotating Designs

## Overview

This activity integrates art with math. Children create rotating designs on paper using the polygons created in the whole class lesson *The Four-Triangle Problem*. (See page 16.) The results are often quite beautiful. Students post the designs and the shapes they used for others to examine. For experience with spatial visualization, children examine one another's designs and guess which shapes were used to create them.

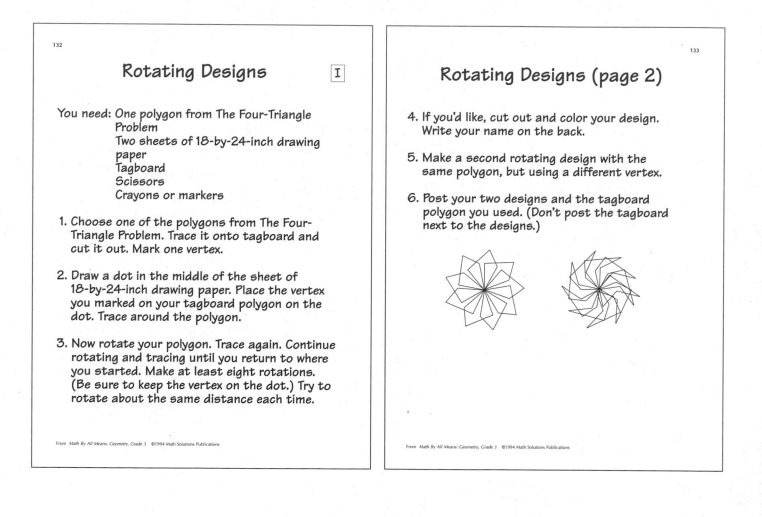

---

132

### Rotating Designs   I

You need: One polygon from The Four-Triangle
        Problem
        Two sheets of 18-by-24-inch drawing
        paper
        Tagboard
        Scissors
        Crayons or markers

1. Choose one of the polygons from The Four-Triangle Problem. Trace it onto tagboard and cut it out. Mark one vertex.

2. Draw a dot in the middle of the sheet of 18-by-24-inch drawing paper. Place the vertex you marked on your tagboard polygon on the dot. Trace around the polygon.

3. Now rotate your polygon. Trace again. Continue rotating and tracing until you return to where you started. Make at least eight rotations. (Be sure to keep the vertex on the dot.) Try to rotate about the same distance each time.

From *Math By All Means: Geometry, Grade 3*  ©1994 Math Solutions Publications

---

133

### Rotating Designs (page 2)

4. If you'd like, cut out and color your design. Write your name on the back.

5. Make a second rotating design with the same polygon, but using a different vertex.

6. Post your two designs and the tagboard polygon you used. (Don't post the tagboard next to the designs.)

From *Math By All Means: Geometry, Grade 3*  ©1994 Math Solutions Publications

## Before the lesson

Gather these materials:
- White drawing paper, 18-by-24-inch, two per student and three extra for samples
- Markers or crayons
- Scissors
- Polygons from the whole class lesson *The Four-Triangle Problem* (See page 16.)
- Tagboard
- Blackline masters of menu activity, pages 132–133
- Two sample rotating designs made by following the directions on the menu activity (Use a different four-triangle polygon for each design.)

## Getting started

■ Post the two designs you made. Ask the students to guess which polygons you used for your completed designs. Have all who volunteer explain their thinking; encourage them to use the shapes to test their ideas.

■ Demonstrate how to make the designs, using one of the tagboard templates shapes from your designs but marking a different vertex. Trace and rotate several times until you think that the children understand the method.

■ Explain that the students are to choose one polygon and use it to create two rotating designs. They trace the polygon they chose onto tagboard and cut it out. Then, for each design, they use a different vertex to place on the center dot. Point out that for each design the children should try to rotate the same distance each time and rotate the polygon at least eight times.

■ If they'd like, students may color and cut out their designs. Ask them to post their designs and tagboard templates so that later other students can try matching templates with designs.

■ In a later class discussion, ask students what similarities and differences they notice among the designs. Then ask children to try to match each design with a template. Encourage them to explain their predictions.

## FROM THE CLASSROOM

To prepare for this lesson, I chose two of the 14 four-triangle polygons. On separate sheets of drawing paper, I traced and rotated around the dot I had drawn. On one design, I traced and rotated 8 times; for the other, I made 15 rotations. I wanted the children to see different examples because I knew that when only one example for an art activity is given, students often try to imitate it. I posted my designs and the templates I had used.

"Those are really cool, Mrs. Rectanus," said George enthusiastically. "Can we make some too?"

"Of course," I laughed, and said, "These are called 'Rotating Designs,' which is the name of the next menu task. In this activity, you create designs by rotating a polygon around a dot and tracing the polygon each time you rotate it. What do you think I mean by 'rotating design'? Talk with someone sitting near you."

A few minutes later, I asked for the children's attention and called on Drew. "The designs you made all look like circles around the outside," he said.

"They're not perfect circles though," added Emma, "because they all have jagged corners or angles."

"What does rotate mean?" I asked. Students began talking with one another.

After a couple of minutes, I called the children to attention. David volunteered first. "Rotating is when something goes around, like a Ferris wheel or the earth," he said.

I called on Alex next. "Records on a record player rotate too," he said, "and we rotate in P.E. when we play volleyball. My mom has a chair that rotates. Lots of things rotate."

"Like footballs and baseballs and basketballs," Noah called out.

Julie added, "The other day, my mom took the car in to have them rotate the tires."

"You're quite observant," I told the class. "What do you think rotate means?"

Courtney raised her hand. "I think it means to go around," she said. More than half of the class nodded or murmured agreement.

"Go around what?" I pushed.

The class was quiet. I waited for the children to think about my question, and then I asked them to talk to their neighbors about their ideas.

Finally, Justin asked tentatively, "Does it mean to go around a *center* of something?"

"Tell me more," I said.

"Well," Justin continued, beginning to sound more confident, "like with wheels. They have spokes that all go into the middle. And planets, they all rotate around the sun, and it's the *center* of the solar system." Justin knew a lot about the world and loved sharing his knowledge with others.

"I get it," said Noah. "Things have to rotate around a center. Otherwise they'd just be rotating around . . . nothing!" he finished.

"Does someone have a different idea?" I asked.

No one else did, but Tanya offered to look up "rotate" in the dictionary. With some help from Jenny, Tanya found the appropriate page and read aloud the various definitions. We talked about the definitions and the difference between revolving and alternating, which Alex had alluded to in his P.E. example and Courtney in her tire rotation example.

**NOTE** Probing children's thoughts not only has the potential to reveal more about their ideas but also gives students the message that you are interested in their thinking and you value their ideas.

Next, I presented the directions on the menu task to explain how to begin making a rotating design. "Choose a polygon that you like from *The Four-Triangle Problem* and get a large piece of drawing paper," I told the class.

I demonstrated as I gave the directions. "Next, take a piece of tagboard, trace around the perimeter of your four-triangle polygon, and cut it out. The tagboard is easier to trace than construction paper." The children watched intently as I demonstrated how to trace and cut out the shape.

"Then choose a vertex of your tagboard polygon and mark a dot on it so you remember which one you chose," I said. When giving these directions, I purposely used the words "perimeter," "polygon," and "vertex" to help children become more familiar with the standard terminology.

I marked a vertex on my template and posted my drawing paper on the chalkboard so they could see as I traced and rotated. "Make a dot close to the center of the drawing paper. Then place the shape on your paper so that the vertex touches the dot. Trace around the shape." I traced the hexagon I had chosen.

"Here's where the rotating part comes in," I said. "I'm going to rotate my shape a little bit. But I'm also going to make sure that the vertex still touches the center dot on my paper. Then I'll trace again." I modeled my instructions.

Immediately five or six children raised their hands.

"Does it matter how much you rotate your shape?" asked Tom, who loved to be neat and precise when drawing.

"It's really up to you," I replied. "If you only rotate your polygon a little bit, it will take you longer to complete your design. If you rotate your design a lot, you'll finish quickly, but your design might not look as interesting." I traced examples of each scenario quickly on the chalkboard to demonstrate what I meant.

"You should rotate the polygon at least eight times," I continued. "For each rotation, I'm going to try to rotate the polygon the same distance, so I have the same opening each time." I rotated and traced twice more to be sure the children understood.

"When you have finished your first design," I explained, "take a second piece of paper and make another rotating design, using the same template. But for the second design, choose a different vertex. Mark it with a different kind of dot from the one you used for the first design."

"Can we color our designs when we're through?" asked Edward.

"Yes," I answered, "and you can cut them out, if you like."

To prepare children for the follow-up discussion to this activity, I directed their attention to the two finished samples I had made and the two templates I had used. "I used one of these shapes for each design," I said. "Can you tell which shape I used for each?" The children looked carefully.

**NOTE** As often as possible, introduce or reinforce the use of correct geometric terminology. Children learn best from repeated experience in the contexts of their learning activities. Also, concrete references help students become more familiar with the words.

Noah's hand shot up. "You used the hexagon for that one on the top," he said. "I'm sure of it."

"How could you convince us?" I said.

"Can I come up?" he said. I nodded yes. Noah took the template and positioned it with the marked vertex on my dot to show how it fit my tracings.

"Can I show the other one?" Kendra asked. I said yes, and she demonstrated as Noah had.

I then gave the final directions. "Post both of your completed designs on the bulletin board and post your template in a different place on the bulletin board. When everyone has made two, we'll talk about our designs and see if we can figure out which templates were used for which designs."

There were no further questions. Almost all the children decided to try *Rotating Designs* first when they went to work on the menu.

Noah's template was a pentagon.

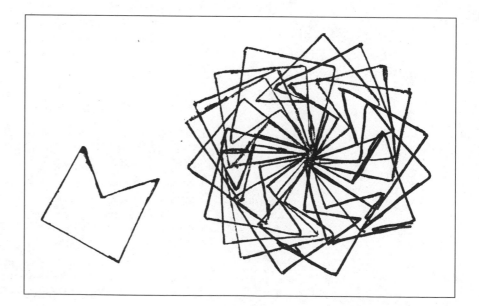

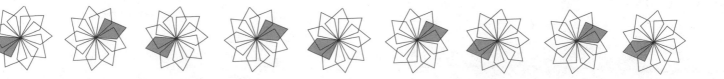

### Observing the Children

As I watched the class work, I was interested to see that some of the children found the task very easy to do. These students traced and cut out their tagboard shapes neatly and quickly and used a consistent measurement when rotating them

Other children, however, found the task difficult. Gordon, for example, had a hard time keeping his shape steady while he traced it. I suggested that he use a masking tape loop to hold the shape in place as he traced. As Gordon went to get the tape, the fire alarm went off. "Oh no," Gordon groaned as he got in line, "Now I'll never be able to remember where to trace next!"

"I'll help you, Gordon," offered Edward.

When we returned to the classroom, Edward went over to Gordon's desk. He glanced at Gordon's drawing for a second or two, then pointed and said, "You need to put the shape right here and trace." I was impressed that Edward saw so easily where to continue, especially since Gordon's paper was covered with many shaky lines and erasures.

After completing her second design, Kendra asked me, "Can I do another and use a circle instead of a four-triangle shape? I have a picture in my mind about what kind of design I'd get using a circle, and I want to try it."

"That's fine," I told Kendra. "What do you think it will look like?" Kendra sketched a design on a piece of scratch paper to show me and went off to try out her idea.

The *Rotating Designs* activity was a popular menu choice over the next few weeks. Even after we finished the unit, *Rotating Designs* continued to be a favorite free-time activity.

Kendra was pleased with the star-like design her hexagon template produced.

### A Class Discussion

The bulletin board was filled with templates and colorful rotating designs. I gathered the class for a discussion. Children pointed to designs and talked excitedly about them with one another.

I called for the students' attention and asked, "What do you notice about the designs?" About 15 hands shot up.

"They're beautiful!" exclaimed Timmy.

"And colorful," added Nicole.

"I like the one that Craig did, the red and black spiral," said Gordon.

Felicia chimed in, "When I was working, I thought I messed up really bad, but when I was finished and colored my design, you couldn't even tell where I messed up! I liked doing this because no matter what you do, the designs still end up beautiful." I heard many murmurs of agreement.

"What do you see about the designs that is the same or different?" I asked.

The children looked carefully at the designs for a few moments, and then Paul commented, "All of the designs have pointy corners, except for that round one." He pointed to the design Kendra had made.

"How did someone get a circle?" Justin asked indignantly. "I didn't think you could get a round design because all the shapes we used have sides and corners!"

"I made it," Kendra giggled. "I traced a masking tape loop and used it for my design." She pointed to her template.

"How did you know where to rotate?" Justin demanded.

"Easy," replied Kendra. "I just put a dot on the outside of the circle template I made and used that." Justin looked fascinated and upset.

"I wish I'd thought of that," he said, chagrined.

Alex commented, "I notice that all the designs use different colors."

Edward used 27 rotations for his design.

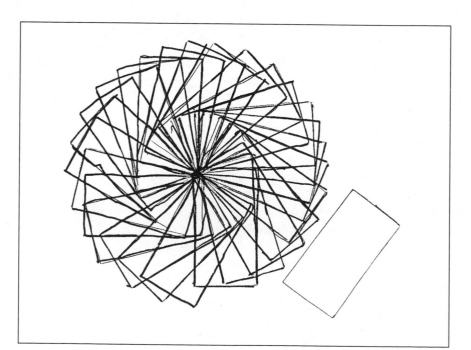

"And different numbers of spaces between the lines," added Elena. "See, look at the pink and purple one. It has a lot of space between the tracings. But Edward's black and red one only has a little bit of space between each tracing. Boy, didn't your arm get tired?" she asked Edward, who blushed proudly and shook his head. Edward frequently was sensitive to others' feelings and went out of his way to protect his peers. Yet when others paid attention to him, he often looked embarrassed.

After everyone who wanted to had made a comment about the shapes, I pointed to one of Lisa's designs and said, "Take a look at this design Lisa made. Which template do you think she used to make it?" The children began talking to one another.

After a few moments, I called on Julie. "I think she used the square," said Julie.

"Why do you think so?" I asked.

"Well, when you look at the design, the pink and purple lines look like they make squares," Julie replied.

"She's right!" cried several children. Julie unpinned the square from the bulletin board and matched it to Lisa's design.

"Do mine next," pleaded George. I nodded. George unpinned one of his designs and held it up for everyone to see. George's design was multi-colored, and it was difficult to discern the shape he had used. The class became quiet as they tried visually to match the correct template to George's design.

Nicole recorded the number of times she rotated the triangle.

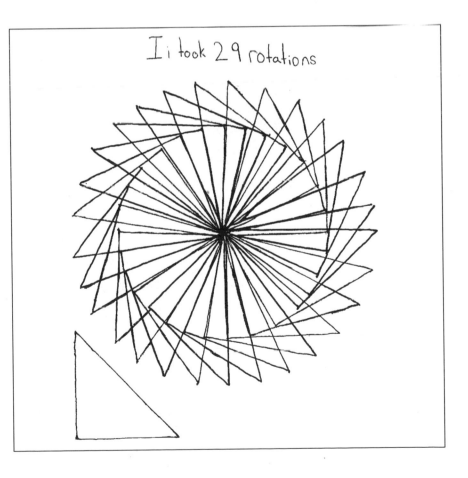

I i took 29 rotations

   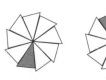

**NOTE** Different activities interest different children. Also, not all students will derive the same benefit from each activity. It's important to decide when to move on and how to offer options to those who are interested in continuing with an activity.

Finally Jenny said, "Is it the rectangle?" She tried the shape, and it didn't match.

"Try the hexagon that looks like the state of California," Paul suggested. Being closest to that template, Alex unpinned it and held it against George's design.

"It matches!" cried several children when Sara traced her finger along the outline of the template on the design.

After about 10 more minutes in which we matched five more designs and templates, several students were losing interest. I decided not to continue the discussion with the whole class and encouraged children who were still interested to try matching other templates with designs.

## MENU ACTIVITY

## Four-Triangle Color Arrangements

### Overview

*Four-Triangle Color Arrangements* extends students' experience in the whole class lesson *The Four-Triangle Problem* (See page 16.) The activity provides children with another experience to develop their spatial problem-solving ability. Students choose one of the four-triangle polygons and explore different ways to make it using two triangles of one color and two of another. The students try to find all of the possible arrangements.

---

134

# Four-Triangle Color Arrangements $\boxed{\text{P}}$

You need: Polygons from The Four-Triangle Problem
          3-inch paper squares in two colors
          One sheet of 18-by-24-inch newsprint
          Scissors
          Tape or glue

1. Cut one 3-inch square of each color on the diagonal into two triangles.

2. Choose one polygon. Arrange the four triangles to make the polygon you chose. Record your arrangement by taping or gluing your triangles onto newsprint.

3. Cut two more squares into triangles and find another color arrangement for the polygon you chose. Tape or glue it onto the newsprint. Continue cutting and arranging triangles to find all the possible arrangements.

4. Post your work.

From *Math By All Means: Geometry, Grade 3* ©1994 Math Solutions Publications

---

## Before the lesson

Gather these materials:
- Sets of four-triangle polygons the students made in the whole class lesson *The Four-Triangle Problem* (See page 16.)
- About 300 3-inch construction paper squares of two contrasting colors (Avoid red and green together, in case you have students who are color blind.)
- 18-by-24-inch newsprint, one sheet for each pair of students
- Scissors
- Glue or tape
- Blackline master of menu activity, page 134

## Getting started

■ Direct the students' attention to the polygon graph of four-triangle shapes. Point to the triangle, and ask students how they might describe the color arrangement in it. Encourage all who volunteer to offer their ideas.

■ Ask students to look at the triangle in their set of four-triangle polygons and decide if the color arrangement is the same as or different from the triangle on the class graph. Have someone from each group report and show the group's triangle to the class for the rest of the students to verify. Have students post triangles that are different from the one on the graph or from the others posted.

■ After all groups have reported, ask the children whether other color arrangements exist for the triangle. Have students who find other arrangements post them for the class to check.

■ Talk with the students about how they might be sure when they've found all the possible color arrangements and how they might convince someone else. Important: Be sure to discuss what makes color arrangements different. For example, if two polygons have the same color arrangement when one is flipped, are these the same or different?

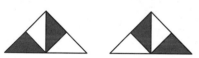

If two polygons have the same color arrangement, but triangles are positioned in different ways, are these the same or different?

There's no right answer to these questions, but the students should agree on one convention to follow so that they are all thinking similarly about what makes color arrangements the same.

■ Introduce the menu activity. Explain that students are to work in pairs, choose a four-triangle polygon other than the triangle, and find all the color arrangements using two triangles each of two colors. To keep a record, they tape or glue the triangles onto newsprint. When students think they've found all the arrangements, they should post their work.

**NOTE** While some mathematical ideas are based on logical relationships, others are arbitrary conventions that call for agreement. No existing mathematical rule defines when color arrangements of four-triangle shapes count as the same or different. Therefore, the students must decide. There isn't a right or wrong decision; what's important is that the students' definition is clear enough for them to use and comprehensive enough to classify all examples.

## FROM THE CLASSROOM

After distributing the envelopes of four-triangle polygons to the students, I pointed to the triangle on our polygon graph. "Who can describe how the blue and green triangles are arranged to make the triangle?" I asked. "Talk it over with your neighbor."

After a few minutes, I called on Tom. "The two blue triangles make a triangle," he said. "So do the green ones. Then the two triangles were put together."

"Check the triangle your group made," I instructed. "Did you make it the same way as this one, or are the colors arranged differently?"

"Ours is the same," Kendra said. I asked her to bring it up, and I posted it on the board.

Timmy raised his hand and said, "Ours is different. It goes green, blue, green, blue."

He pointed to the alternating colors. I asked Timmy to post his group's triangle next to Kendra's.

Nicole said, "Ours is like Timmy's, except it goes blue, green, blue, green."

She posted her triangle next to the other two.

Gordon added, "Ours is like the first one, but backwards." He pinned his group's triangle on the bulletin board. "See?" he said, showing how the colors were reversed.

Tanya interjected, "But flip it, and it's the same. So it doesn't count."

"But it looks different," Gordon said, defending his triangle.

"Timmy's can be flipped to match Nicole's," Craig called out. "So it shouldn't count either." Discussion broke out among the children. I called them back to attention.

"Which is right?" Edward asked me.

"We'll have to decide together," I answered. "There's no mathematical rule about this, but we all have to agree so we're thinking the same way. The question is: If a color arrangement looks different, but you can rotate or flip it to match an arrangement you already have, should it count as the same or different?"

Several children called out, expressing their opinions. Obviously, some had strong opinions. I called them back to attention. "One at a time," I said. "Remember to raise your hand."

I called on Kendra. "I think they should be the same," she said, "because they were the same when we flipped them to find different shapes."

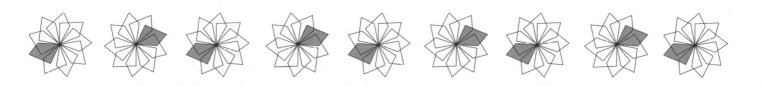

"But this is different," Gordon said. "If they look different, they should count."

Again, several children began to talk at once. I quieted them and asked them to discuss the question in their groups. "Then we'll decide as a class," I said.

After a few minutes, I asked for their opinions. All the groups reported they had decided on Kendra's position that the arrangements were the same.

"How do you feel about this?" I asked Gordon.

"It kind of makes sense," he conceded.

"So what do we do?" I asked, referring to the triangles that were posted.

"I'll take ours back," Nicole said.

"Me too," Gordon said.

I removed their triangles and returned them. It would have been all right with me if the class had come to a different decision. Or if they hadn't all agreed, we would have continued discussing it until we came to a decision.

"What other color arrangements are there for the triangle?" I then asked. "Have the group supplies person get squares, scissors, and tape, and see what you can find." The children began moving around paper triangles on their tables, searching for arrangements and talking among themselves. I circulated and observed them working.

After a few minutes, I asked for their attention. "Let's post any new color arrangements you've found," I said.

Five students posted triangles. Three were new arrangements. The triangles posted by Grant and Lisa, however, opened up another discussion about same and different.

Their color arrangements were the same, but they had each positioned two triangles in a different way to make the square inside. After some discussion, the students decided these were the same. "We're supposed to pay attention to the colors, not the lines," Emma said.

"We have a different one," George said. "It's a blue parallelogram with a green triangle on top and a green triangle stuck to the side!"

"I think you could do it the other way with a green parallelogram," Emma mused.

Finally, we agreed that there were six different color arrangements for the triangle.

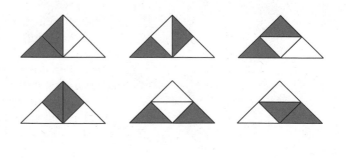

### Introducing the Activity

I showed the students the menu task and explained what they were to do. "For this activity," I said, "choose a partner, pick one of the other polygons on the graph, and find all the different color arrangements for it, just as we did for the triangle. You can glue or tape your shapes to a piece of newsprint or make a drawing of your arrangement. When you think you've found all the possibilities, post your work."

My classroom procedure was that children could choose their own partners. Students knew that partners were expected to work together, sharing the work and the recording. I had told the class at the beginning of the year that they could continue to choose their partners as long as partners actually worked with each other and did not fool around. If I saw partners whose actions showed me that they couldn't handle the responsibility of working together, I separated them and did not let them work together again during the unit. After I had separated several partners early on in the school year, the class learned that I meant what I said and that I followed through consistently.

I had planned to introduce the *Same and Different* menu task at the same time as this one, but since our beginning discussion had taken so long, I decided to have all of the children work on this activity. They would be able to make choices after I introduced another menu activity.

### Observing the Children

Students immediately got to work. I observed their interactions as they searched for the different color arrangements. Tom and Edward chose to work together, and they found all the color arrangements for three shapes in the same time it took other groups to explore only one shape.

Gena seemed disinterested in the task. She sharpened her pencil several times, used the bathroom twice, and went for a drink of water several times during the half hour that the children worked on the task. Despite those interruptions, Gena's partner, Nicole, seemed happy to be her partner. I walked with Gena to the water fountain during one of her trips. "I notice that you're avoiding doing the work with Nicole," I told her gently. "Why?"

"Well, it's sort of hard for me to find them, and I don't want Nicole to think I'm dumb," she responded.

"Having difficulty seeing the color arrangements doesn't make a person dumb," I told Gena. "It just means that you probably haven't had many opportunities to do activities like this. You just need more experiences with geometry and more time to make sense of things." I reminded her of learning to ride a bike. "We have trouble at first sometimes," I said, "and then with more experience, we became more confident and it becomes easier." Gena seemed reassured and headed back to Nicole, a determined look on her face.

Mark and Gordon, who had had a disagreement earlier in the day, chose to be partners but had a difficult time agreeing on which shape to explore and how to divide the work. It was a good reminder for me to be aware that children's emotions can affect learning and that creating and sustaining an environment in which students can work together is important.

By the end of the period, three pairs of students had posted their results. The others hadn't finished and continued work on other days. Over the

**NOTE** Teachers use different methods to arrange students into pairs or groups. Some teachers assign students, some randomly arrange pairs or groups, and others allow children to make the decisions. There's no one best system, but the system used must be clear to the students.

next week, I encouraged students to look at the work as it was posted. I noticed that the students who were most interested in spatial puzzles of this kind were the most diligent about examining other arrangements and talking about missing and congruent arrangements.

I decided not to have a formal class discussion about this activity. I wasn't interested in making sure that each pair had found all the possible arrangements for a shape. Instead, I wanted to provide students with the opportunity to explore possibilities and talk with their partners about the arrangements they created. These kinds of conversations help children become comfortable with using geometric terminology. Also, I respected that some children were more interested than others in this activity. I believed that the activity introduction had served as an in-depth discussion about the exploration.

# ASSESSMENT Polygon Cards

**FROM THE CLASSROOM**

Teachers can learn about what students understand about properties of polygons by asking children to make polygon cards. On a 3-by-5-inch index card, children draw a polygon of their choice. On the back of the card, they record all the words and phrases they can think of to describe the polygon. Finally, on the front of the card they draw the same number of lines as words or phrases on the back.

You can gain insights into children's thinking both by talking with them as they create their polygon cards and by reading what they've written on their cards.

Polygon cards can later be put in a box for others to solve during menu time. Children look at the polygon on a card, count the number of lines on the front of the card, and try to guess the words or phrases written on the back to describe the polygon. They record their guesses, then turn over the card to check.

About halfway through the unit, I started class one day by calling the children to the rug.

"I'm interested in learning what you know about polygons," I began. "In a few minutes, I'll give each of you a 3-by-5-inch index card. On the front of the card, you'll draw a polygon. On the back, you'll list all the words or phrases you can think of to describe your polygon. Next, on the front of the card you'll draw the same number of lines as words or phrases you wrote on the back. Later, we'll use your polygon cards for puzzles. Other students will look at the polygon you drew and the number of lines on the front of the card and guess the words or phrases you used to describe the polygon."

I showed the class the front of the index card I had prepared. I had drawn a rectangle, positioning it on a tilt so that the sides weren't parallel to the edges of the card. Too often, children see shapes pictured in only one way, and I tilted the rectangle to encourage flexibility. Next to the rectangle I had drawn 10 lines, one for each word or phrase I had written on the back to describe the rectangle.

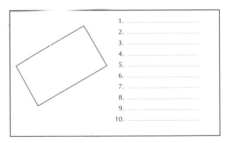

On the back, I had written:

polygon, quadrilateral, parallelogram, rectangle, four sides, four angles, all angles are right angles, two lines of symmetry, opposite sides are parallel, opposite sides are equal

"What words or phrases do you think I wrote to describe this shape?" I asked. "Talk about this with your neighbor." There was much talking

and gesturing. After a few minutes, I asked the children for their attention and called on Elena.

"Rectangle," she said. I recorded her word on the board.

Gena volunteered next. "You could have written 'quadrilateral!'" she said triumphantly. I wrote her suggestion under Elena's.

"Polygon!" shouted Noah, unable to keep quiet any longer. I wrote his suggestion under Gena's.

Kendra said, "You could write 'square corners,'" and several students nodded agreement.

"Has a line of symmetry!" shouted Noah again. I added Kendra's and Noah's suggestions.

Paul said quietly, "Actually, you should say it has two lines of symmetry." He came to the front of the room and traced his finger on the card to indicate the lines of symmetry. I changed Noah's suggestion so it read "has two lines of symmetry."

After Paul sat down, the class was momentarily quiet. Then Lisa offered, "Has four sides," leading Tanya to add, "and four angles—four *right* angles!"

I doubted that all the students knew what right angles were, so I said to Tanya, "Tell us what you mean by 'right angles.'"

"They're angles that have square corners," she answered. "Like if you took something square and put it inside the angle and lined it all up, the lines would match the square corner." She demonstrated by drawing a rectangle on the board and then holding up a book to show that it fit exactly inside one angle. "But I don't know why it's called a 'right' angle," she finished, and sat down.

"I don't know either," I replied. "I've asked several people and looked in several books, but I haven't found the answer yet. I'm still trying to find out." The children seemed impressed to hear me admit that I didn't know. It's good for children to see teachers as learners.

I recorded Lisa's and Tanya's suggestions. I had written 10 words or phrases to describe the rectangle, and the children had made 7 suggestions. After a minute or so of silence, Justin said excitedly, "Rectangles have parallel lines!"

As I recorded Justin's suggestion on the board, Grant groaned and remarked, "Oh, *I* should have noticed that!" Grant remembered the conversation he had had with Justin and Cal about parallel lines when I introduced the menu activity *Same and Different.* (See pages 64–65.)

I waited a bit, but the students had nothing further to add. "Let me write my list on the board," I said. The children made comments as I recorded my words and phrases. "Oooh, we got that one." "She counted angles and right angles as different." "Parallelogram? How can a rectangle be a parallelogram?" "Oh, look, opposite sides are equal. We should have gotten that one." "We did pretty good."

"Any questions?" I asked.

"Does Justin's count?" Edward asked.

"What do you mean?" I asked.

"Well, it's really the same as yours," he explained, "but different." Justin had suggested "Rectangles have parallel lines" and I had written "opposite sides parallel."

"What you do think?" I asked the class.

"I think they're the same," Kendra said, "just different words. But they mean the same thing."

"Does it count?" Edward persisted.

"I agree with Kendra," I answered. "Justin and I had the same idea."

"I don't get 'parallelogram,'" David said, stumbling over the word.

"Well, a rectangle is a special kind of parallelogram," I explained. "They both are quadrilaterals with opposite sides parallel, but a rectangle has the extra feature of having all square corners, or right angles, as Tanya called them." David seemed satisfied, but I wasn't sure he understood the classification system. This didn't trouble me. The classification of polygons is complicated, and I expect children to learn at different rates.

I then told the children, "Now it's your turn. Choose any polygon you like and draw it on an index card. On the back, write all the words and phrases you can think of to describe it. On the front, draw the same number of lines as there are words or phrases on the back. When you can't think of anything else to add, bring your card to me. Then you can choose an activity from the menu."

Alex asked, "Does it have to be a polygon from the four-triangle problem or can we choose any polygon?"

"Draw any polygon you like," I responded.

### Observing the Children

While the children worked, I circulated among them, observing and discussing their work. Felicia called me over to show that she had used a ruler to draw a 2-inch square.

"I'm really proud that I got all the sides exactly 2 inches long," she said, a smile lighting her face.

Nicole struggled with drawing a rectangle. She had difficulty making right angles. Edward, who was sitting nearby, noticed her difficulty and suggested, "Try using two edges of the card for two sides of your rectangle. Then you only have to draw two more sides. See? Like this." He drew an example on the back of his card.

"Oh yeah, cool!" replied Nicole, and she tried again.

Alex was bent over his card in apparent fascination. Curious, I went over to find out what he found so interesting. He had covered the card with triangles.

"Tell me about your card," I said.

Alex replied excitedly, "I've been drawing all sorts of polygons with three sides and three corners, and did you know that every single one of them is a triangle?"

Alex was delighted with his discovery and eager to share it. "Hey look, George," he said, taking his card over to George's desk. "Did you know that every shape with three sides and three corners is a triangle?"

George studied the paper for a moment, cocked his head to one side and said, "Huh. That's neat," and he promptly went back to work. Alex rushed over to tell Sara and Lisa.

In the meantime, Ben brought me his card. On the front, he had drawn an equilateral triangle and seven lines.

On the back, he had written: *triangle, polygon, 3 sides, 3 corners, no right angels, oppisite sides equal, oppisite angels the same.*

Ben described an equilateral triangle seven ways.

"Would you have written the same things if you had drawn this?" I asked, drawing an isosceles triangle on the board. Ben studied it for a few moments and then said, "Maybe I want to add a few things to my card," and he returned to his seat.

As I circulated, I found it necessary to encourage some children. Julie seemed to have a difficult time recording her thinking. Being aware of her difficulty with processing and expressing language, I had encouraged her to use a tape recorder, a tool she uses occasionally. On the front of her card, Julie had drawn a regular pentagon with four lines below it. Then she came to me for help spelling a few words for the instructions she was writing underneath the four lines: *Turn on the tape recorder for my words about this shape. Julie.* She then began speaking confidently into the tape recorder. "My first line would have the word 'pentagon' written on it. Did you figure it out? Good. My second line is the word 'polygon.' I bet you got that one . . ." I left as she continued to record.

Tanya could only find two words to describe the irregular pentagon she drew.

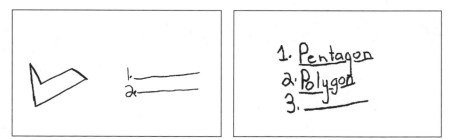

Timmy spent a great deal of time drawing a shape. "I want it to have all the sides the same," he told me. Timmy was carefully using a straight edge to measure 1-inch sides. I was interested in what he knew about measurement.

"Tell me about your polygon, Timmy," I said.

"Okay," he replied happily. "First, I thought about what polygon I wanted to draw, and since 12 is my favorite number, I decided to make a dodecagon, since dodecagons have 12 sides and 12 corners. Then I knew I wanted the sides to be the same length, 'cause it would look neat." Timmy was invested in neatness and precision in his work.

Timmy continued, "I suppose the sides wouldn't have to be the same length. Anyway, I wanted to use a ruler so the sides would be straight. I knew I couldn't make longer sides 'cause then the dodecagon wouldn't fit on the card. But when I started to measure and draw, I saw that my dodecagon wouldn't be able to look . . . you know, kinda round like a head of a nut that you use with a wrench, because the card is too small.

So, instead of using a measurement smaller than an inch, since I don't know how to measure anything smaller than an inch, I decided to make a polygon that wandered around the card. I came up with a decagon."

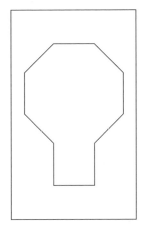

I was interested to learn that, while Timmy indicated he had preferred to draw a regular dodecagon, he was able to draw an alternative that would fit on the index card. I noticed that many students' polygons, including Timmy's, had a line of symmetry. I wondered why so many children drew symmetrical polygons.

Gena worked for about 30 minutes before bringing her card to me. She had traced a trapezoid from the pattern blocks and drawn eight lines next to her drawing. She said to me with excitement, "I worked for a long time, and I thought really hard. Every time I thought I was done, I thought of something new to say about it. This was fun!" She had written: *trapezoid, polygon, 4 sides, 2 paralel sides, no symetry, no right angls, no congrunt sides, quadrilateral.*

Gena rarely stayed engaged with a task for long, and I was surprised to see how much time she had spent on the assignment. It was a powerful reminder for me that children have different experiences with the same activity, and that students have differing levels of interest.

"Gena, tell me what you mean when you say that every time you thought you were done you thought of something new to say about your trapezoid," I said.

"Well," Gena began, "after I wrote 'polygon,' I started thinking about trapezoids, and I knew they had four sides. So I wrote that. Then I thought about what Grant said the other day about parallel lines, and I noticed that my shape had two. Then I thought that because my shape had parallel sides, that it should have symmetry too, but when I looked at it carefully, I saw that it didn't have any symmetry. So I wrote about that. I thought I was done then, but I thought, if it doesn't have symmetry, is there anything else it doesn't have? And I realized about right angles and congruent sides. Finally I looked at the four-triangle chart and saw that a trapezoid is a quadrilateral. When I wrote that, I knew I was done!"

"I'm curious about how you decided that your trapezoid wasn't symmetrical," I said, "because I notice a line of symmetry."

"You do? Let me look again," she replied, and she stared at the shape she had drawn. After a few moments, she said, "You're right! There's a line right down the middle." Gena substituted the word 'has' for 'no' in her phrase *no symetry*.

**NOTE** Symmetry is a geometric property that students seem to understand easily, almost naturally, because there are so many examples in the world around them. The word "symmetry" names an idea with which children are already familiar, and therefore the mathematical terminology seems easy for them to remember because it connects with their own experiences.

Gena's explanation helped me realize how important it is to focus on the process of thinking about mathematics as well as the outcome of that thinking. By interacting with the children as they worked, my understanding of their thinking was much deeper than if I had simply read their cards.

Gena found eight ways to describe the Pattern Block trapezoid she traced.

For his card, Craig had drawn a circle. "I know you said to draw a polygon, but I just couldn't resist." He grinned as he showed me the circle with six lines drawn neatly beside it. Craig had written: *circle, not a polygon, no sides, no corners, only made with points, looks like a cookie.*

Later, when we shared the polygon cards, several children commented that they liked Craig's shape best because it was original and reminded them of cookies, one of their favorite things to eat. This led to an interesting discussion of the shape of foods, how and why they are packaged in certain ways, and what this means for the consumer. I was interested that the children saw some connections between geometry and the real world.

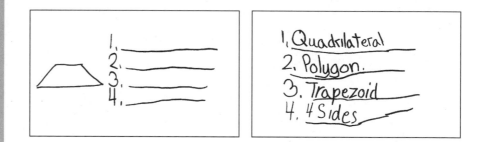

Sara also drew a trapezoid, but listed only four ways to describe it.

Over the next few days, all students who wanted to share their cards with the class did so, and interested students such as Gena and Timmy continued making other polygon cards during menu time.

I collected the students' cards and put them in a box on the shelf where we kept our math manipulatives. I told the children that they could look at the cards during menu time. "If you have suggestions about words or phrases someone could add," I said, "then be sure to talk with the person about your ideas."

## MENU ACTIVITY

### Overview

### The Put-in-Order Problem

This activity extends the whole class lesson *Toothpick Patterns* (see page 34) and provides experience with spatial visualization, congruence, and mirror and rotational symmetry. Children arrange the toothpick cards they created in the earlier lesson into a line so that each pattern displayed can be changed to the next one by moving just one toothpick. As an extension, students solve the additional problem of arranging their cards in a continuous loop following the same rule.

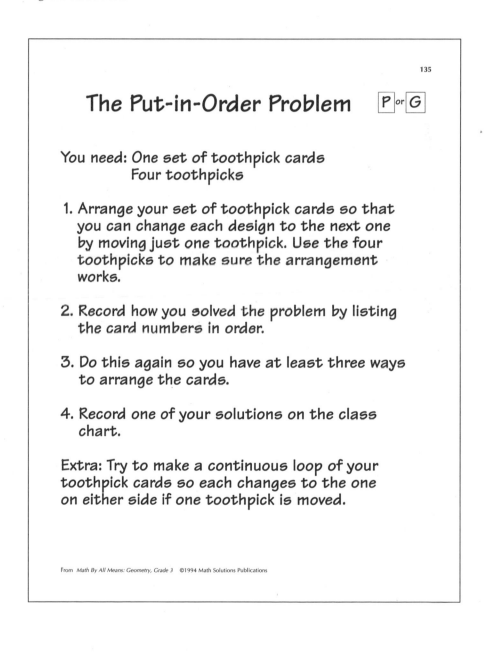

135

# The Put-in-Order Problem  P or G

You need: One set of toothpick cards
Four toothpicks

1. Arrange your set of toothpick cards so that you can change each design to the next one by moving just one toothpick. Use the four toothpicks to make sure the arrangement works.

2. Record how you solved the problem by listing the card numbers in order.

3. Do this again so you have at least three ways to arrange the cards.

4. Record one of your solutions on the class chart.

Extra: Try to make a continuous loop of your toothpick cards so each changes to the one on either side if one toothpick is moved.

From *Math By All Means: Geometry, Grade 3*  ©1994 Math Solutions Publications

## Before the lesson

Gather these materials:
- ■ Toothpick playing cards from the whole class lesson *Toothpick Patterns* (See page 34.)
- ■ Toothpicks
- ■ One sheet of chart paper labeled "The Put-in-Order Problem"
- ■ Blackline master of *Put-in-Order Problem Samples*, page 136
- ■ Blackline master of menu activity, page 135

## Getting started

■ Tell the children that they will work in pairs or groups to arrange their toothpick cards in a line, following the rule that each pattern can be changed into the next one by moving just one toothpick.

■ Make one of the toothpick patterns, using the overhead projector or building the pattern on one desk and having the class gather around. Ask the students to visualize toothpick patterns that could be made by moving just one toothpick. Let children with suggestions try their ideas by moving a toothpick. (It might be helpful to students if you post one group's set of toothpick arrangements from the whole class lesson *Toothpick Patterns.*)

■ The blackline master of *Put-in-Order Problem Samples* shows two possible ways to begin making the toothpick patterns, one that is correct and one that has an error. Have students look at and discuss these two patterns with their partners or groups.

■ When you are satisfied that students understand the procedure of moving a toothpick to change one pattern into another, tell them that they are to arrange all the cards in order by following the same rule, then record the order they use. Explain that they are to find three different arrangements.

■ Post the sheet of chart paper with the title "The Put-in-Order Problem." Tell students that once they've recorded their three ways, they should pick one sequence and record it on the chart. Tell the students to record only sequences that haven't already been written on the chart.

■ In a later class discussion, ask students to explain the strategies they used to solve the problem. Also, ask them to see if they notice any patterns in the arrangements on the class chart.

## FROM THE CLASSROOM

To introduce the activity, I arranged four toothpicks on the overhead projector.

The toothpick arrangements Kendra's group had made were posted on the bulletin board where the students could easily see them.

"I made the J pattern on the overhead projector," I told the class. "What patterns could I change it into by moving just one toothpick? Talk about this to someone sitting nearby." I chose the J pattern because it could be changed into all but three of the other patterns.

Several students offered solutions. "Try the letter F." "You can make the box." "You can make the Little Dipper." "I think you can make number 9." Children with suggestions came up to the overhead to try their ideas.

Then I explained the menu activity to the students. "In this activity, you can work in pairs or in a group. Begin by placing one of the toothpick cards face up in front of you and building the pattern with toothpicks. Then talk about the other toothpick arrangements you could change it into by moving only one toothpick, as we just did with the letter J.

"Decide on one arrangement and change your original pattern by moving a toothpick. Then find the matching card and place it face up next to the original card. Continue in this way until all the cards are in a row in front of you, and you're sure that each pattern can be made from the previous design by moving just one toothpick. You may have to do some rearranging in your line to make it work. When you agree that you've found a way to order all the cards, use the numbers on the cards to record the order on a piece of paper. Then mix up the cards, choose a new card to start with, and try it again."

Justin commented, "This is like the toothpick game, except a little different. You still look at the cards and move things around, but you record something different."

"Yes, the activity is like the toothpick game," I agreed. "But this time, if you reach a stalemate, you can try to rearrange cards so you use them all. Any other comments or questions?" The children were silent until Ben raised his hand.

"Can we start?" he asked.

I laughed and replied, "Sure, as soon as I give you your last two instructions. When you've found and recorded three different ways to arrange the cards, choose one and record it on the class chart. Make sure the way you choose is different from the others posted." I posted the sheet of chart paper I had titled "The Put-in-Order Problem."

"Finally," I continued, "for an extra challenge, try to arrange the cards in a continuous loop that follows the same rule."

"Oh I get it," Nicole interrupted me. "You find a way to put the cards in a circle, so when you put the last card down, it sits next to the first card, and you can make the last into the first card by changing just one toothpick!" She took a deck of cards and immediately started to arrange the cards in a loop. Sara and Grant quickly joined her.

The students had no other questions, and they began working on the menu.

## Observing the Children

Usually when I introduce a new menu activity, many of the children choose it during menu time, but today was an exception. Most went back to work on *Rotating Shapes*. Nicole, Sara, and Ben, however, worked on *The Put-in-Order Problem* with obvious delight.

"I love a challenge!" Nicole enthusiastically informed me. The trio rapidly changed one design to another until they came to the last card, the straight line. It couldn't be made from the previous pattern, the box. The three children looked at one another and began giggling.

"Oh no," said Ben, laughing. "It doesn't fit. What are we gonna do?"

After the group had stopped laughing, Sara said in a serious voice, "Does this mean we have to start over?"

At the same time, though, Nicole was looking at the cards already laid in a row. She moved several around. I asked her what she was doing.

"I'm trying to see if I can trade the straight line with another card in the row so it will work," she answered.

"Good idea!" cried Ben, and the three began in earnest to find a card to trade with card number 10. After a few minutes, the three students looked up at me in exasperation. Their cards were in disarray.

"Let's start again and use the straight line design for our first card. Then we won't have to worry about trying to fit it in at the end," said Nicole, and the group went back to work.

Gena and Justin were also working on the problem. They called me over to where they were working. Gena was holding card number 3, the box shape, in her hand.

Justin said, "We got to the end of the row, and the box was our last card. It doesn't fit because you can't change the plus sign into it. We tried and tried, but we don't know how to make it work."

"How about trying to fit it between other cards in the line?" I suggested.

"You mean we can do that?" asked Gena incredulously. "I thought it was cheating."

"No, it's not cheating and yes, you can do it," I smiled at them.

As it turned out, almost every group ran into that same problem at some point when working on the activity. I found it helpful to refer children to Gena, Justin, and other children who had already encountered the problem.

Ben and Nicole started each of their lines with cards 13 and 9. They also solved the extension problem of arranging the cards into a loop.

Put-In Order Problem

1. 13, 9, 4, 5, 11, 3, 15, 16, 6, 7, 8, 10, 12, 14, 2, and 1.

2. 13, 9, 5, 11, 3, 15, 16, 6, 7, 8, 10, 12, 14, 2, 1, and 4.

3. 13, 9, 5, 11, 13, 15, 6, 7, 8, 10, 12, 14, 2, 1, 4 and 16.

LOOP: 13, 15, 16, 4, 1, 9, 2, 5, 14, 11, 12, 3, 6, 7, 8, 10,

**A Class Discussion**

By the following week, all the students had tried *The Put-in-Order Problem* and recorded their sequences on the class chart.

> ## The Put-in-Order Problem
> 3/16/ 2/ 12/ 4/ 1/ 9/ 11/ 5/
> 10/8/7/14/6/13/15
> ___
> 2/13/15/3/16/6/14/7/8/10/1/11/9/12/ 4/5
> ___
> 11,5,12,14,6,13,15,3,16,10,8,7,4,1,2,9
> ___
> 14/6/16/2/1/5/10/11/3/15/13/9/4/7/8
> ___
> 8,10,16,3,6,15,2,13,9,4,5,11,7,1,12,14
> ___
> 8,7,10,12,4,1,16,6,14,2,11,5,9,13,15,3,
> ___
> 15,3,16,11,5,1,2,6,12,14,7,8,10,4,9,3
> ___
> 9,13,15,3,16,11,5,1,2,6,12,14,7,8,10,4,
> ___
> 8,10,5,4,12,14,7,6,11,15,3,6,2,1,9,13
> ___
> 3□,|1|,||,16,15,|4,12,|5,4,2,
> 14,7,8,9,4,M,13
> ___
> 1,2,14,6,13,16,3,15,11,9,10,8,7,12,5,4,
> ___
> 1-2-11-7-8-10-16-3-16-4-13-6-14-12-5-4
> ___
> 1,3,9,5,11,3,15,16,6,7,8,10,12,14,2,1, and 4
> ___
> 16,6,9,1,12,14,7,4,5,11,3,15,13,2,10,8
> ___
> 8,7,9,6,3,15,13,2,11,4,10,1,12,14,16,5

To begin class one day, I asked the class to look for patterns on the chart. The children studied the chart intently. After a while, Justin raised his hand excitedly.

"I see a pattern!" he announced. "Except for Drew and Edward, and Gena and me, everyone put cards 8 and 10 next to each other." He came to the chart and pointed out the 8 and 10 on each list.

"Which cards are those?" I asked.

"The straight line and the tall L, " several children said.

"We changed the straight line to the line with one toothpick sticking straight out, number 7, and so did Drew and Edward," Justin finished triumphantly and sat down.

"What patterns can you change the straight line into?" I asked.

After a few moments, children called out several responses. "Number 10." "Number 7." "Number 8."

"Are those the only possibilities?" I asked.

I called on Courtney. She came to the board and drew the straight line, then drew the design on card 10 to the left of it and the design on card 7 to the right.

"These are the only possibilities," she said. "All the other patterns need more moves." She demonstrated with several cards.

Tom and Timmy found that card 8, the straight line, could only fit between cards 10 and 7.

The Put-in-Order Problem

15/11/12/14/16/2/7/8/10/1/4/5/9/13/6
3

13/2/6/3/15/11/5/9/10/8/7/6/14/12/14

2/13/15/3/16/6/14/7/8/10/1/11/9/12

4/5

Timmy raised his hand. "3 and 15 are next to each other a lot," he said.

"And 11 is next to 3 and 15 a lot too!" added Jenny. She went to the board and drew the three patterns.

"They work together no matter what order you put them in. They were good ones to use for the loop," she said.

The class began looking for other combinations of patterns that worked in the same way. The students looked at the beginning and ending card in each line, but didn't find any patterns. The discussion lasted about 15 minutes. The children were actively involved, looking for patterns and proving or disproving one another's conjectures.

Later, when I looked again at the class set of papers, I noticed several cards that were frequently used to begin or end the line. In the future, I plan to have students record on the class chart all three ways they solve the task instead of just one, so we'll have more data to examine. Also, I'll ask students to write about the problems they encountered and their reactions to the activity.

Mark and Cal drew their patterns as well as indicating their numbers.

# MENU ACTIVITY

## Square Up

### Overview

The game of *Square Up* draws from the mathematical areas of geometry and logic. Playing the game gives children practice with spatial visualization and also provides experience with strategic thinking. Players take turns placing colored markers on geoboard pegs, trying to mark four pegs that define a square. After playing the game many times, students write about the strategies they used.

---

137

## Square Up  ⃞P

You need: One geoboard
One rubber band
Game markers with holes, 12 each of
two colors
Geoboard dot paper

1. Each player uses a different color marker. Take turns placing a marker on a peg of the geoboard. The object is to place four of your color markers to mark the corners of a square.

2. When you think four of your markers mark the corners of a square, say, "Square Up." The other player says, "Prove it." Prove it by stretching a rubber band around the pegs you think are the corners of a square.

3. If a player has made a square, the game is over. If not, keep playing until one player makes a square or all the pegs are covered.

4. When the game is over, record on geoboard dot paper where you each placed your markers. Play again.

From *Math By All Means: Geometry, Grade 3*   ©1994 Math Solutions Publications

## Before the lesson

Gather these materials:
■ Geoboards
■ Rubber bands
■ Game markers in two colors that have a hole in them, such as Two-Color Counters with holes, Unifix Cubes, or 1-inch squares of construction paper with holes punched in the middle
■ Geoboard dot paper (See Blackline Masters section, page 140.)
■ Crayons or markers
■ Blackline master of menu activity, page 137

## Getting started

■ Tell children that you are going to teach them a two-person game called *Square Up.* Have one student read the rules on the menu task as you model playing with another student. The rest of the class can gather around to watch or, if possible, you can use a transparent geoboard on the overhead projector.

■ When you've finished playing one game, show the children how to record the results by using two different color crayons or markers on geoboard dot paper.

■ After the students have had time to play the game over several days or longer, initiate a class discussion about the strategies they used. Then have children write about their strategies. (If the students haven't yet formed strategies, postpone the writing assignment until they've had more experience playing the game. Then have another class discussion before asking them to write.)

## FROM THE CLASSROOM

I gathered the children on the rug and said, "I'd like a volunteer to help me teach a new game." More than half of the students raised their hands, and I chose Kendra.

"This game is called 'Square Up,'" I said. "To play, you need one geoboard and one rubber band." The children had had experience with geoboards early in the school year. If they hadn't previously explored and become familiar with them, I would have provided time for free play before asking the students to use the geoboards for a game.

"Also, you each need 13 markers," I continued. "We'll use the Two-Color Counters with holes in them. One player uses the red side and the other uses yellow." I counted out 13 for each of us.

"Would someone like to read the directions from the menu task?" I then asked. I chose David and asked him to read the first direction.

"*Each player uses a different color marker,*" he read.

"Which color would you like to use," I asked Kendra, "red or yellow?" Kendra chose yellow.

David continued reading. "*Take turns placing a marker on a peg of the geoboard. The object is to place four of your color markers on pegs to mark the corners of a square.*"

"Let's each place a few markers," I said to Kendra. "You can go first." Kendra and I each placed three markers. My third play blocked Kendra from making a square with her next move but put me in a position so that I could make a square on my next move.

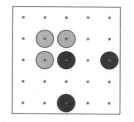

I stopped to let David continue reading.

*"When you think four of your markers mark the corners of a square, say, 'Square Up,'"* he read. *"The other player says, 'Prove it.' Prove it by stretching a rubber band around the pegs you think are corners of a square."*

"I get it," Craig said. "You have to try to make a square, but you try and block the other person."

"Look," Justin noticed, "Mrs. Rectanus almost has one."

"Oooh, Kendra," Emma warned, "you'd better put one in the right place."

Kendra looked intently at the board, while the others shouted suggestions. Kendra was having trouble focusing with all the hubbub. I quieted the class and asked Kendra if she would like help from someone.

Kendra was silent for a minute. "No," she said, finally spotting where she had to play to block me. She placed one of her markers, and the students cheered. I played another marker, again setting myself up to make a square. However, the square I was working toward didn't have sides parallel to the sides of the geoboard, and I knew from experience that children just learning the game probably wouldn't notice it.

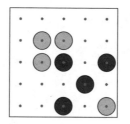

I was right. Kendra played a marker that didn't block me but set herself up for a win.

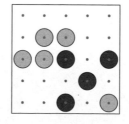

I played my marker and said, "Square Up!"

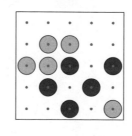

The class looked at the board incredulously.

"Who remembers what the other player says when one says, 'Square Up?'" I asked.

"Prove it!" several children called out. I stretched the rubber band around the four pegs I had marked.

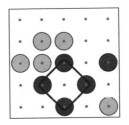

"That's not a square," Tom said. "It's a diamond."

"Oh, yes it is," Lisa said. "It's on a slant." Several children burst out laughing.

"That's pretty tricky," Gordon said.

"I didn't know you could do it that way," Courtney said.

"Wow!" Kendra said. "I didn't see that."

"Read the rest of the directions," I said to David.

He read, *"If a player has made a square, the game is over. If not, keep playing until one player makes a square or all the pegs are covered."* David stopped and looked at me.

"If I hadn't been able to prove I made a square," I explained, "then we'd keep on playing. Read the rest, David."

*"When the game is over, record on geoboard dot paper how you each placed your markers,"* David read.

I took a sheet of geoboard dot paper and showed the class how to record Kendra's and my plays with red and yellow crayons. "You can use this one sheet to record nine games," I pointed out.

"How many games do we play?" George asked.

"As many as you'd like," I said. "The idea of the game is to help you develop sharp eyes for noticing squares. The game can help you learn to think geometrically. After a few days, we'll talk about the strategies you found to make squares."

There were no other questions, so the children began work on the menu.

**NOTE** When teaching a competitive game, keep the focus on its educational value. In this instance, children should be told that the purpose of the game is to develop their geometric ability, not just to win.

### Observing the Children

About two-thirds of the class chose to play *Square Up* that day. Many continued to play over the next week, some choosing to play during recess. All of the children seemed to enjoy the game, but they differed in their ability to visualize squares. While some children made squares easily, others had difficulty noticing opportunities or seeing when to block their opponents.

When I observed children recording their finished games, I also noticed differences. While some children easily placed the marks on the geoboard dot paper, others had difficulty matching the pegs on the geoboard to the dots on the paper. I encouraged children to help one another to be sure their records were accurate.

Children kept records on geoboard dot paper. The last game shows that Sara missed saying "Square Up."

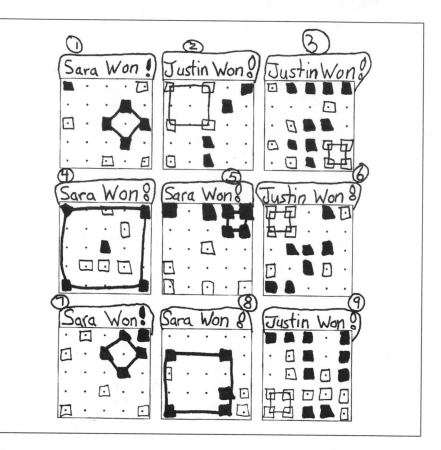

### A Class Discussion

After about a week, I initiated a class discussion about the children's strategies. "What kinds of strategies did you use to make squares or stop your partner from blocking you?" I asked. I waited to give children time to think. I began by calling on Mark.

"I tried to make big squares, not small ones," he said. "I think they're harder to spot."

"I made squares like a diamond," Emma said.

"What do you mean, 'like a diamond?'" I probed.

"You know," she said, "the slanty kind." Others children murmured that this was a good idea.

"Oh, so the sides aren't parallel to the sides of the geoboard," I said, using the geometric terminology. "Any other ideas?"

"Don't look where you are trying to make a square," Timmy said. "Don't give them a hint."

"Yes," Lisa concurred, "try and concentrate somewhere else."

"You have to be sneaky," Tom added. Others nodded. This was a popular strategy.

"Sometimes it's good to waste a move just to throw them off the track," Justin said.

"That's how he beat me," Grant grinned.

"Block their move and try and win at the same time," Ben said. I had noticed that Ben was a very savvy player.

"Play lots in the middle so they think that's where you're going, and then make a square at the side," Tanya said.

Lisa described six approaches.

#1. I hide a square so it can't be seen.

#2. I make it diaganle.

#3. I pretend to try to make little squares and distract my partner. Then I pretend to try to make little squares in the corners.

#4. I don't make little squares, because they're to clear.

#5. I take the middle spot. It's easy to get squares there.

#6. I pretend to consontrate on a place while I'm really making a square somewhere else.

"I try and make an L," Courtney said. "Then I can make a square next."

I was surprised at the range of ideas. "I want to be able to remember all you told me," I said, "so I'd like each of you to write all the strategies you can think of to make squares. You can write about any ideas you thought of or any you heard from others today that make sense to you. Try and write as much as possible."

Felicia, who doesn't like to write, used illustrations to explain her strategies.

Square-Up

If you make a square like this: It is very easy to win

**The Children's Writing**

Most children wrote quite a bit about their strategies. I think that the class discussion was helpful preparation for this assignment.

Ben, who was particularly adept at playing, explained his strategies: *Try to get squares that are in a diangle* [diagonal] *or a diamond. Waste one cube to make them think you are doing a bad move then you have a chance of winning. Block their move and try to win at the same time. Try to win and consentrate your hardest.*

Courtney explained her theory about making an "L." She wrote: *Make a L, but start at the ends, not the middle part. They won't reconize the L yet and go somewhere else. Then you make the L complete. They will like the L so much they won't notice the saquare and go somewhere else again. Then you win!!*

Craig wrote: *1. If you would distrac them like if they make a bad move say "No No don't come here" they would go there anyway. 2. Try and make Big! and little ones sideways. 3. I made almost five ways so when they block it I would do it in another place.*

In his paper, Noah listed six strategies: *1. I would make big squares not small. 2. Make squares like a dimond. 3. Make squares at the corners. 4. talk to your partner. 5. Try to sneek in a extra square. 6. pretend to say were you are not going to go. 7. If you are loosing make a cat's game.*

Noah had learned to force a tie game when he was losing.

---

Square Up Stratages

1. I would make big squares not small.

2. Make squares like a dimond.

3 Make squares at the corners.

4. talk to your partner.

5. Try to sneek in a extra square.

6 pretend to say were you are not going to go.

7. If you are loosing make a cat's game.

Rachel had chosen not to explain her strategies in the class discussion. "I didn't want to give it away," she said. She wrote: *#1. If you make a T it dose'ent matter were they go. You will win! #2. If you make a sqare in teh corner it is harder to see. #3. If you are working on two sqares it is easyer to win.*

Rachel's first strategy gave her a back-up plan for being blocked.

Sqare-up Strategies

#1. If you make a T it dose'ent matter
were they go. You will win!
#2, If you make a sqare in the corner
it is harder to see.
#3 If you are working on two sqares
It is easyer to win.

# MENU ACTIVITY

## Covering Boxes

### Overview

This activity extends the whole class lesson *Investigating Boxes*. (See page 46.) Each child chooses a box, covers its congruent faces with the same color construction paper, and glues yarn of the same color to all of the same-length edges. The activity offers children experience with measuring area and length; contributes to their mathematical understanding of shape, size, congruence, and similarity; and provides opportunities to discuss mathematical terminology.

---

138

## Covering Boxes    I

You need: One box
            Construction paper
            Colored yarn in two or three colors
            Glue
            Scissors

1. Glue construction paper to each face of your box. Use the same color for all congruent faces. Try to cover your box neatly.

2. Once you have covered the faces, glue yarn on the edges. Use the same color yarn for edges that are the same length.

From *Math By All Means: Geometry, Grade 3* ©1994 Math Solutions Publications

---

## Before the lesson

Gather these materials:
- Boxes from the whole class lesson *Investigating Boxes* (See page 46.)
- Construction paper, 12-by-18-inch or larger, in at least three colors
- Skeins of thick yarn in at least three colors
- Scissors
- Glue
- Rulers
- Blackline master of menu activity, page 138
- A box that is a rectangular prism, covered according to the directions on the menu activity (Glue colored paper to each face, following the rule that all congruent faces must be covered with the same color paper. Then glue yarn on each edge, using the same color yarn for edges that are the same length.)

## Getting started

■ Show the class the box you prepared. Ask them how many faces the box has. Point to sets of congruent faces and ask: "Why do you think I covered these faces with the same color paper?" If no one guesses correctly, explain that the faces with the same color paper glued to them are congruent. Review that "congruent" means exactly the same size and shape.

■ Ask the students how many edges the box has and have them guess why you glued the same color yarn on some. Measure with a ruler to prove that some edges are the same length. Ask: "How many vertices are there altogether on the box?" If needed, review that vertices are corners. Count with the children to verify.

■ Review the mathematical names for your box—polyhedron and rectangular prism. Remind students that polygons are two-dimensional shapes with straight edges and polyhedra are three-dimensional solids. Tell them that "poly" means many. If you'd like, introduce names for different polyhedra: tetrahedron (having 4 faces), pentahedron (5 faces), hexahedron (6 faces), heptahedron (7 faces), octahedron (8 faces), decahedron (10 faces), and dodecahedron (12 faces). Add these words to the Geometry Words chart.

■ Introduce the menu task. The instructions on the menu direct students to follow the same procedure you explained. Ask: "What are some ways to cut the paper and yarn so that they fit exactly on the faces and edges?" Discuss.

■ After all children have completed the task, begin a class discussion. Make sure everyone can see the completed boxes. Ask questions and let all children who want to share do so. Encourage the students to listen to one another's ideas. Below are some questions you might ask during the class discussion:

"How did you do the task?"

"What was hardest about doing this activity? Easiest?"

"What did you learn while doing the task?"

"How did you help one another?"

"What did you like about the activity? What did you dislike?"

**NOTE** What a student gets out of a class discussion differs for each child. Asking a range of questions maximizes children's chances to participate and helps teachers learn about children's understanding.

# FROM THE CLASSROOM

To prepare for this lesson, I covered the faces of a family-size cereal box with construction paper, using orange for the two faces with the greatest surface area, turquoise for the two congruent side faces, and green for the top and bottom of the box. I glued red yarn along the length of the four long congruent edges, black yarn on the four shortest congruent edges, and white yarn on the other four congruent edges.

"I've covered this cereal box with construction paper and glued yarn on the edges," I told the students. "Why do you think I covered these two faces with orange paper?" I asked, pointing to the faces.

Several children raised their hands. I called on Nicole. "I think you covered them with the same color paper because they're on opposite sides," she said. "One's on top and one's on the bottom."

"Yes, that's true," I responded. "Does anyone have a different idea?" I called on David.

"They're the same size," he said.

"And the same shape!" added Justin.

"Yes, that's why I chose to cover them with the same color paper. Both faces are exactly the same size and shape," I replied.

"They're congruent," said Kendra.

"They are," I confirmed. "What about these two faces that are covered with turquoise paper? Why did I choose the same color paper for them?"

Almost every student in the class raised a hand. "They're congruent!" many children called out.

"How do you know for sure that the turquoise faces are congruent?" I asked. The children began talking to one another.

"If you measured them you'd see that they have the same measurements," offered Gordon.

"How would you measure them?" I asked.

Gordon went to get a 12-inch ruler and returned to the rug. He held the ruler up to one turquoise face so that the 12-inch mark was lined up with one edge and about 3 inches of the ruler protruded beyond the other end. "It's 12 inches," he said.

"No, no!" cried several children.

"Huh?" asked Gordon, surprised.

"You need to line up the end of the ruler where the *first* inch is with the end of the box, not the *last* inch," said Jenny. She got up and demonstrated how to use the ruler correctly. "It's almost 9 inches long," she finished, and sat down.

"Oh, I get it," replied Gordon, and he measured both dimensions of the face correctly. "This one is 9 inches by 3 inches, and . . ." Gordon fumbled with the ruler and then measured the opposite turquoise face. "It's the same!" he said triumphantly and sat down. Several children applauded.

"Does someone have a different way to check if the faces are congruent?" I asked.

After a moment, Lisa volunteered. "You could trace around one of them on a piece of paper, then put the other on what you traced and trace around it. If the shapes you trace are the same, then the faces are congruent," she finished softly.

"You could just kind of look and see," offered Timmy.

The children didn't volunteer any other ways to check for congruency, so I asked, "How many faces are on my box altogether?"

"Six." "Four." "Eight." There were a variety of responses. Even though we had spent a good deal of time on the activities in the *Investigating Boxes* whole class lesson, not all children knew the number of faces on boxes. Children often need a great deal of experience to learn new ideas.

Alex said, "Look, there are two orange faces, two turquoise, and two green. That's two, four, six."

"He's right," said Julie. She touched each face as she counted it, and many students nodded in agreement.

"What about the edges? How many edges are there on my box?" I asked.

There was silence for a moment, as many children pointed and counted softly to themselves.

"12," several children said. Nicole took the box and counted the edges slowly.

"Why do you think I covered these edges with red yarn?" I asked the children as I pointed to the edges.

"It's the same reason as the faces," Edward said patiently. "They're congruent." He took the box and Gordon's ruler and measured the length of each.

"You don't need to measure all of them," said Grant. "If the length of the longest face is 9 inches, then the length of the edge will be the same. It's obvious." Edward looked crestfallen.

"Grant," Gena interjected, "maybe it isn't obvious to Edward."

Grant looked embarrassed, and said, "Sorry Edward."

I was surprised by Grant's observation. I hadn't expected anyone to notice that. It was a good reminder for me that children are capable of more than we sometimes give them credit for.

"How many vertices are there altogether on the box?" I asked next.

Again there was silence as the children counted. The range of answers was from 4 to 10.

"Look," said Gena decisively, "There are eight." She counted the corners carefully.

"Mathematicians call one corner a vertex," I reminded the children. "All corners together are called vertices."

Tanya raised her hand and said, "That's nice that corners have a special name. Vertices. I like that on something ordinary like a box there are all kinds of special names for things—faces, edges, vertices."

"Me too," said Julie.

"You know," said Paul in his quiet, thoughtful way, "if the cereal box were squashed flat it would be a rectangle and would have four corners—er, vertices. But because it's three-dimensional, it has twice that, or eight corners."

I was interested in Paul's reasoning and wanted to find out more. "Would your conjecture hold for any kind of box?" I asked him.

He replied, "Well, I don't know, but I think so. Except for the oatmeal box, I guess. For an oatmeal box you can't tell how many corners it has because where the round part meets the lid is one big corner."

"An oatmeal box is called a cylinder," I said, "and I understand why you might think it has one big corner. For something two-dimensional, like a polygon, a corner is made where two lines or sides meet, and we call it a vertex. On a three-dimensional object, a corner or vertex is where three or more faces come together." I wrote the word "cylinder" on the Geometry

Words chart. "How many faces do you think a cylinder has?" I asked as I picked up the oatmeal box and rotated it slowly for the children to see.

"Two!" several children shouted.

"No, three!" said Emma. Her group had worked with an oatmeal box in the tracing faces activity during the *Investigating Boxes* whole class lesson. "If you take off the lid and cut right down the box to the bottom with a straight line, cut off the bottom like the top lid and unroll the box, you'll have three pieces, the lid, the bottom, and the big rectangular piece. So it's got to be three. Do you understand?" she asked the class.

Several students looked confused and shook their heads.

"Can I cut it apart?" Emma asked me.

"Yes," I said. Emma got a large pair of scissors and proceeded to cut the box with help from Tanya and Grant. It made sense to sacrifice one of the oatmeal boxes to provide physical proof of Emma's idea. Emma held up the pieces for everyone to see.

"Oh, okay, I get it now," said Alex, who had looked confused initially.

"If the definition of a vertex is the point where three or more faces meet or intersect, where do the three faces of the cylinder meet?" I asked.

"They don't," Cal said.

"So does that mean that an oatmeal box only has two corners?" Noah wanted to know.

"Tell me more about your question, Noah," I said. "What do you mean by corner?" I wanted to find out more about Noah's thinking.

"Well, a corner is where two things meet. Like when you go down to the corner of Wildwood and Oakland Avenue, you turn left to go to the freeway," he finished.

"Can someone explain why it might seem like the oatmeal box has two corners?" I asked.

"Sure," said Ben. "You get one corner where the rectangular face meets the lid, and the other where it meets the bottom."

Knowing that terminology is not always standard in our language, I understood why some of the children were confused. I realized that Noah's and Ben's confusion was a natural part of the learning process, yet I was at a loss for what to say to them. It seemed inappropriate to continue to repeat or rephrase the mathematical definition of a vertex.

"What do you think about Ben's and Noah's ideas?" I asked the class. "Talk to your neighbor about it."

After a few minutes of conversation, I called on Tom.

"You just have to remember that a corner on a box is where *three* faces come together. I don't know what you call the place where *two* faces come together, though," he commented.

"Let's look at the box I covered with paper and see," I said. I touched an orange face and an adjacent green face, sliding my fingers toward one another until they met at the edge of the box.

"An edge!" seven or eight children cried excitedly.

"I think I get it," said Ben, a bit uncertainly.

"It's okay if you're confused about this," I told the students. "We often need many experiences with an idea before we really understand it. We all learn things at different times and in different ways." Ben looked relieved.

"How do you think I accomplished the task of covering the faces and edges of my box with yarn and construction paper?" I asked.

**NOTE** Verifying hypotheses with physical objects can help students make abstract ideas more concrete. The more experience children have with concrete materials, the more likely they are to develop understanding of geometric relationships.

**NOTE** It supports children to let them know that partial understanding and confusion are natural to the learning process and that people learn at different rates.

"Maybe you measured each face and cut out a piece of paper that size," suggested Elena.

"Or maybe you traced the faces and cut," said Craig.

"You could have just looked at the face and guessed what size paper you needed," said Timmy, repeating his earlier idea.

"For the edges you can cut a length that you need and then use that piece as a model for the other pieces," Courtney said.

"Or measure them with a ruler," Nichole offered.

After every child with an idea had volunteered, I introduced the menu task. I didn't specify how I wanted each child to accomplish the task of covering a box; I left that challenge for the students. Also, I decided to use the menu item as an informal way to assess the children's understanding of geometry and measurement concepts.

### Observing the Children

The students approached the problem in many different ways. Some children took a great deal of care in covering their boxes. Other students, such as George, did not.

I couldn't tell how George decided which faces were congruent on his shoe box, but he followed the directions and covered the congruent faces with the same color paper. However, he cut the paper haphazardly, and it didn't fit; it hung off one edge and didn't entirely cover the faces. Some of his yarn was cut too long and hung off the box. Glue was everywhere. George didn't seem to mind.

When I asked him how he knew what size paper to cut and how long the yarn needed to be, George replied brightly, "Oh, I like Timmy's idea of eyeballing it. I can just tell what sizes I need. This is fun!"

Felicia, on the other hand, wanted her paper pieces to fit exactly. She carefully traced one face of her shirt box onto construction paper, cut it out, and then used the cutout as a template for the second piece. She checked each piece before gluing it, trimming where necessary. She methodically covered all the faces before working on the edges.

Nicole covered two faces of her box and then glued yarn where appropriate. She ran into trouble, though, when she tried to glue the next two pieces of paper to the box. The yarn got in the way, and Nicole became frustrated. I didn't interfere but let her figure out how to solve the problem.

After about 10 minutes, I called for the children's attention, even though not everyone had chosen to work on *Covering Boxes* during menu time. I wanted some children to share their approaches with the class so that others would see a variety of options for solving the problem.

"I realize that not everyone is working on *Covering Boxes*," I said. "However, can anyone comment on something you've learned about the activity that might help others when they work on it?"

Nicole immediately cried out, "Do all the paper first or you'll *never* get it right!"

Jenny said, "I found out that you can trace a face, fold the paper underneath your tracing, and cut it out. Then you'll get two pieces exactly the same size."

"If the paper doesn't move when you're cutting it," added Craig, chagrined. "I thought it was a great idea until I tried it."

Mark commented, "I traced a face, then put a second piece of construction paper the same color under my tracing and taped them together. Then I cut like Jenny. It's working pretty good."

The students went back to work, many spending the rest of the math period on the task.

### A Class Discussion

I waited until all the students had completed the task before starting a class discussion. I began by asking students how they had approached the task. After about half the students had raised their hands, I called on Justin.

"I used the paper to help me cut," he began. "I took my tissue box and lined it up on the corner of the paper, so I only had to trace along two edges. That way I ended up with straighter lines."

"Good idea!" several children murmured.

Cal said, "Tom and I worked together. I held the box while he traced around it. We didn't mess up that way."

Several other students volunteered their methods. Then I asked, "What was difficult about this activity?"

It seemed as if everyone started talking at once. "Share your thoughts with a neighbor, and then we'll share as a whole class," I instructed. After about two minutes, I called for attention.

"Tracing the box was hardest," said Elena.

"You should have tried my way. I just looked and estimated," offered George.

Elena looked at George's box and said, "No thanks." George shrugged and smiled.

"Cutting the paper," said Drew. "It kept slipping."

"Getting the right size paper was hardest for me," added Maurice. "I tried to measure it with a ruler, but I kept getting the wrong measurements, and then I got confused."

"What did you do then?" I asked him.

"Justin helped me," he replied.

"How did Justin help?" I wondered.

"Instead of using a ruler, I told Maurice to hold his box along two edges and then trace the other two. He tried it and it worked!" Justin explained.

"That's right," Maurice said and smiled.

Gena said, "Doing the oatmeal box was hardest. I couldn't tell where the face began and where it ended." There were murmurs of sympathy from the children.

"How did you deal with that situation, Gena?" I asked.

"Well, Julie showed me how to mark the box where I started," Gena said. "She helped me roll it and trace until I got back to the mark, so I knew I had it right." She held up her cylinder for the class to see.

"I liked doing this!" Jenny volunteered. "It was easy, and the boxes turned out looking great—especially your cylinder, Gena," she finished.

"Thanks," replied Gena. "I like your cube too," she said.

"It's the end of math time," I said, "so we'll end our discussion."

Nicole had one last comment. "They sure look pretty all covered like that." The students looked at our pile of boxes and we shared a quiet moment enjoying the colorful collection.

# ASSESSMENT Box Riddles

**FROM THE CLASSROOM**

Most children love riddles. This assessment takes advantage of children's interest in riddles and asks them to write clues about the boxes they covered with construction paper and yarn in the menu activity *Covering Boxes*. (See page 104.) The riddles they write give insights into their familiarity with properties of geometric solids. Also, the riddles can be used for other students to solve.

To introduce the assessment, choose one of the covered boxes and ask the students to describe it. Let all children who volunteer give their ideas. Then explain to the children that they will individually write clues for riddles about the boxes they covered. Tell them that they will read one another's riddles and try to match the riddles with the boxes.

I showed the children the box I had covered. "What can you say about this box?" I asked.

"It's covered with paper," Courtney said.

"It has four . . . no, six sides . . . I mean faces," Paul said.

"Let's check," I said, and the children counted with me as I pointed to each face.

"They're all rectangles," David said.

"What are all rectangles?" I asked.

"The faces," he answered. I showed the children the faces, and they agreed that they were all rectangles.

"It's kind of a medium-size box," Emma said.

"What do you mean by medium-size?" I probed.

"Well," Emma answered, "it's bigger than some and smaller than some."

"How else could you describe its size?" I asked.

"It's like a shoebox, only not so deep and a little fatter," Mark said.

"It looks like a dictionary would fit inside," Kendra said. She got a dictionary to show what she meant. "Well, it's a little bigger than the dictionary," she added.

"It's about a foot long and only a couple of inches high," Justin said.

"Oh, yeah," George said, "you could check with a ruler." He got a ruler and held it against the length of the box. "It's not a foot long. It's just 11 inches."

"You could measure the other sides, too," Lisa said.

George continued to measure. "It's 9 inches this way, and 3 inches this way, and 11 inches this way, and 3 inches this way, and 9 inches this—"

Elena interrupted him. "You're doing the same thing over and over again," she said. "You only have to do three." Elena found it obvious that the box had three dimensions to measure.

George looked at the box. "Oh, I see," he said.

"Is there anything else you could say about the box?" I asked the class.

"It has eight corners," Alex said. I counted with the students to check Alex's statement.

"There's yarn glued on the edges," Sara said.

"And there are 12 edges altogether," Tom added. We counted again.

The class fell quiet. No one else had any ideas about other ways to describe the box. I decided to introduce the activity.

"In just a minute," I said, "you'll each write a riddle for the box you covered. Your riddle will have clues, just like the descriptions you've been giving for my box. The clues should make it possible for someone else to pick out your box, but they shouldn't make it too easy."

"Is this like the polygon cards?" Craig asked, referring to the earlier assessment.

"What do you think?" I responded.

"I think it is, because we have to write things about our box," he answered.

"But it's different," Maurice added, "because we don't have to guess what someone else wrote, just which box matches."

"Do we each do our own riddle?" Felicia asked.

"Yes," I answered.

"Can I put my clues on the tape recorder?" Julie asked.

"Yes," I answered.

There were no other questions, and the children got to work.

Grant's clues focused on the measurements of the edges.

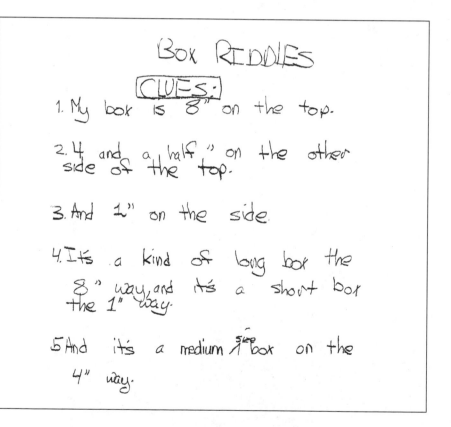

> **BOX RIDDLES**
> **CLUES:**
> 1. My box is 8" on the top.
> 2. 4 and a half " on the other side of the top.
> 3. And 1" on the side.
> 4. It's a kind of long box the 8" way, and it's a short box the 1" way.
> 5. And it's a medium size box on the 4" way.

### Observing the Children

Children approached the task differently. Some focused mainly on measuring the dimensions of their boxes. Jenny, for example, wrote: *1. My box is 11 inches one way and 3 inches the other. 2. There are four 11 x 3 inch faces and two 3 inch square faces. 3. It is one of the longest boxes. Good luck on finding my box!!!!!*

Gena wrote: *1) It is 4¹/₂ inches on the long edge. 2) It is fairly small. 3) It is 1 inch on the small edge.*

When Alex measured two of the dimensions of his box, he was disturbed and came to me for help. "They're not exact," he said.

"Show me what you mean," I responded.

Alex showed me that one side measured between 8 and 9 inches and another between 5 and 6 inches. "See," he said, "they're not exact."

"Oh," I said, "you mean they aren't exactly 8 or 5 inches. They're each a little bit more."

"What do I write?" Alex asked.

"You could write something like 'a little bit more than 8 inches,'" I answered. "Measurement is rarely exact."

"Oh, I know," he said, ignoring my suggestion. "I can write a half." Alex began writing his riddle. He wrote two clues: *1. 8 and a ¹/₂ inches one way and 5 and a ¹/₂ another way. 2. Some of the yarn fell off.* Alex's measurements still weren't exact. Often, children at this age use ¹/₂ to denote any part of a whole; their understanding of fractions is limited.

Kendra came to show me what she had written. "Look," she said, "I measured a different way." Her clues were: *When you turn my box right-side-up it is 5 inches from corner-to-corner. When it is on it's side, it is 3 inches from corner-to-corner. My box is a middle-sized-box. The top is a square, the 3 inch face is rectangle.*

I read her riddle. "I see that you measured the diagonals of two of the faces," I commented.

"Should I write 'diagonal'?" she asked.

"Only if you want to add it," I said.

She thought for a minute. "I'll leave it," she said, and skipped back to her seat.

Some children's clues included properties of the boxes as well as measurements. Rachel, for example, wrote: *Six faces, twelve edges, eight corners. (Getting more impotant.) Parallelepiped, rectangler, one face eight by four inches.*

Kendra measured the diagonals of two faces of her box.

Box Riddles

When you turn my box right-side-up it is 5 inches from corner-to-corner.

When it is on it's side, it is 3 inches from corner-to-corner.

My box is a middle-sized-box.

The top is a square, the 3 inch face is rectangle.

Some children's clues included properties of the boxes as well as measurements. Rachel, for example, wrote: *Six faces, twelve edges, eight corners. (Getting more impotant.) Parallelepiped, rectangler, one face eight by four inches.*

"I put that last one in so they could guess it," she told me.

"Explain what you mean," I said.

"Well," she giggled, "the other clues fit lots of boxes, so I had to give them something special for mine."

Rachel added her last clue to distinguish her box from many of the others.

> ### Box Riddles
> Six faces, twelve edges, eight corners.
>
> (Getting more important.)
> Parallelepiped, rectangler, one face eight
> by four inches.

Jenny's riddle showed that she was able to be more precise about the fractional parts of her measurements than Alex. She wrote four clues: *1. It's not a cube. 2. The longest edge of the largest face is $5\frac{3}{4}$ inches long. 3. The shortest edge of largest face is $4\frac{3}{4}$ inches long. 4. It's a rectangular prism.*

Jenny's riddle shows her comfort with describing fractional parts of inches.

> 1. It's **not** a cube.
> 2. The longest edge of the largest face is $5\frac{3}{4}$ inches long.
> 3. The shortest edge of largest face is $4\frac{3}{4}$ inches long.
> 4. It's a retangular prism.

Sara wrote: *My box is a rectangular prism. It's 7 inches on one side. it's 4 inche's on the other side. The shortest side is 3 inches.*

I was curious about the way Nicole chose to measure her box. She had written three clues: *1. My box is 26 cm. across. 2. And ten inches long. 3. My box is a rectangular prism and a parallelepiped.*

"I noticed that your first two clues give measurements of sides, one in centimeters and one in inches," I responded.

"Oh, yeah. I used the other side of the ruler," she said, showing me how she measured in centimeters. "Justin told me how to write it." What Nicole had done was correct, though unorthodox, and I decided not to talk about the convention of using just one kind of measurement unit.

Mark didn't include specific measurements but identified his box in his first clue. He wrote: *My box is the biggest box and is a rectangular prism. It has 6 faces and 12 edges. All the faces are rectangles.*

Courtney used the colors for most of her clues. She wrote: *Most of the colors are dark. The sides of my box are 8 by 3 and ¹/₂ inches long. There are five colors on the whole box. Ther are 2 colors of string and three colors of paper.*

I posted the children's riddles above the collection of covered boxes. For the next week, interested students gathered there and tried to match boxes with riddles.

# ASSESSMENT What Is Geometry? (Revisited)

Typically, third-grade geometry assessment focuses on children's ability to name polygons and identify geometric relationships. This final assessment is different, however. It focuses on children's overall understanding of geometry, their problem-solving skills, and their reactions to their learning.

In this unit, children actively explored geometric concepts by sorting, classifying, drawing, describing, combining, dividing, and modeling shapes. The activities helped children connect geometry to the real world, develop spatial sense, and relate geometry to number and measurement ideas. In this assessment, students think and write about what they now know about geometry.

To prepare the students for this writing assignment, you may want to have them reread silently what they wrote about geometry at the beginning of the unit. Or, you might just review the menu activities and the materials they used for the activities.

Then ask the children to write everything they know about geometry. Explain that the purpose of the assignment is to help you find out what the students have learned about geometry and what they thought about the unit. Ask the children to be as detailed as possible and write about specific activities they liked and why, what they learned, how their perceptions of geometry changed from the beginning of the unit, and what they think is the value of studying geometry in the third grade.

## FROM THE CLASSROOM

I decided to have the students read the first papers they had written about geometry. I began by explaining the purpose of the assessment.

"When we began this unit, we talked together about geometry and then you wrote about what you knew about geometry. You've all learned a lot since we began, and I'm interested in reading what you know about geometry now. It will help me understand more about you and will also give me information so I'll know if the activities you did could be helpful for teaching other children about geometry." I reviewed the menu items we had worked on and talked briefly about the whole class lessons.

"I'd like you to read the first papers you wrote about geometry and then write what you know now," I explained. "When you write, include how you felt about the unit and what you know now. Add any other information you think will help me understand you and your thinking." I paused for a moment and then asked, "What questions do you have?"

"Does spelling count?" Felicia asked.

"The more accurately you spell, the easier it is for me to read what you're trying to tell me," I replied. "But I'm mostly concerned that you write as much as possible to help me understand what you've learned and how you felt about the unit."

"Can I use the tape recorder?" Julie asked. I nodded.

There were no further questions, and the children fell silent as they reread their original papers and began writing.

As well as learning about geometry, Grant felt he had learned an important social skill.

## What I learned about geometry

Before, I thought I would never understand "Geometry." But now I understand it more evrey day.

I think it's relleay neat how you can make a circle with shapes made out of toothpicks and each one makes one next to it, by just moving one little toothpick.

Not only did I learn about "Geometry" but I learned how to get along with other kids better.

I thought "Geometrcy" was only for odults but now I think it can be for anyone at any time and any age starting at 6.

Kendra wrote: *I learned lots of new geometry words like: 3 dimensional, prism, rectangular prism, faces, vertices/vertix, eges and (my favorite) parrallelepiped. I think 3rd graders should study geometry because you can't teach an old dog new tricks. Geometry is important because theres shapes all around us and if we didn't know what to call them or how to identify them, we would not have strutures, meaning houses, briges, buildings, mostly anything.*

Emma also had a global view of geometry: *I learned that geometry isn't just a bunch of shapes, I understand now that geometry is in everything from the wall of the room to a leftover candy wrapper. I also know that if you aren't persistent with finding shapes you aren't going to find what you want to. I also learned that geometry can be fun for all ages.*

*When you introduced this subject I thought it was going to be imensly boring and not worth while, But now I have a second thought—I noticed that nothing in this class has been boring especially geometry!*

*I also know some thing I didn't know before, that you can turn one shape into another.*

Paul, despite all his verbal insights during discussions, simply wrote: *1. I learned that you can make fourteen shapes out of four triangles. 2. and sixten shapes out of four toothpicks. 3. I learned the names of the shapes from octagon to dodecagon.*

Alex shared his reactions to the unit and his excitement about learning. He wrote: *When I am working on geometry and it's time to clean up, I get upset. Because once I start I get really involved in it! It's because there is oh so much to learn in geometry. It's like space there will always be something to learn! You have to search and search for new things and your bound to find something that nobody has ever found before—like new shapes.*

Many students commented about specific concepts they had learned. Tom wrote: *I learned what convex was. I learned what polygons are. I learned what octagon was and decagon and nongan and concave and a lot more shapes and how they form.*

Justin wrote: *1. I learned that some words mean the same as others, for example, faces and sides. 2. I learned that it's not always best to be alone. A partner sometimes thinks a different way and gets other answers. 3. I learned that learning and experimenting with shapes can be fun. 4. I learned that sometimes you have to think ahead. For instance, in the Put-in-Order Problem you have to say to yourself, "if I put this shape down, can it turn in to this shape?" 5. I learned that you have to look closely at some shapes because they might be congruent.*

Timmy connected what he had learned to the world around him. He wrote: *Imagineing how much shapes in the world would be imposable. There would be at least 30 shapes on one piece of property. And my little house proply has 10,000,000 shapes, I think? I wonder who invented the names for shapes?*

Jenny explained how she changed her mind about mathematics: *I used to think that math was <u>tortcher</u>, but this year, because of the geometry menu, geometry to me is a fun part of math.*

Craig learned a bit about a saying his mother frequently told him. He wrote: *I thought geometry was boring until I did math menu, even though I like nuber's more than shapes. In the put-in-order problem it was hard but me and Maurice stuck to it. When I would sometimes wonder why my mom say stick to it now I know, and I know it helps if you cooperate.*

Jenny was specific about what she had learned—and about how her attitude toward mathematics had changed.

> **What I Learned From the Geometry Menu**
>
> I learned some very interesting geometry words, like: concave, convex, quadrilaterel, perpendicular and so on. I found 5 stratagies for "Square-Up." I learned the names of a: 7 sided shape heptagon, a 9 sided shape nonagon, and a 10 sided shape decagon. I found out that a square is a special kind of rectangle. I used to think that math was ~~tortcher~~, but this year, because of the geometry menu, geometry to me is a fun part of math.

Nicole wrote from a very personal point of view: *I liked the Put-In-Order problem alot because it was hard and it pushed me, like it maked me work hard to get where I was trying to get to and I like that. I think I work better with geometry than numbers because some numbers you have to think of in your head and I don't like thinking of things in my head. I think I do better if the materials that I'm using if there right in front of my face.*

Lisa wrote about her confusion with math: *When I first started 3rd grade I got realy mixed up with geometry and mathematics and I still do get a little mixed up with math and geometry but not so much. I learned: 1. Many shapes can be turned into other shapes with only moving one piece. 2. Math isn't just for adults. 3. Math can be fun. 4. I never knew a diamond can be called a rhombus. 5. never to give up. 6. you need a key two open a locked door.*

Felicia summed up her experience succinctly. She wrote: *I learned that useing my eyes, brain and math things, I could get it all together.*

Sara was extremely enthusiastic about the unit.

> What I learned from the geometry menu
>
> I learned so much! Shapes. geometry. I really liked Rotating Shapes. I dicacoved that shapes are fun, shapes are so, so, so fun. I also dicocovered in ruluting shapes that when you do a shape over and over new shapes start to apear. I love how new shapes apear. I looks like afishal math. It really does. I also learned that four tryangles makes other shapes. Yes. I used to think four tryangles only made a tryangle. That was befor I came in this class ofcourse.
>
> In square up I learned so many difernt ways to make a square. This last menu we just had was my faverit so far. Yes it was.

# CONTENTS

# CHILDREN'S BOOKS

Children's picture books have long been one of teachers' favorite tools for nurturing students' imaginations and helping them develop appreciation for language and art. In the same way, children's books that have a connection to mathematics can help students develop an appreciation for mathematical thinking. They can stimulate students to think and reason mathematically and help them experience the wonder possible in mathematical problem solving.

Each children's book described in this section can add a special element to one or more of the activities in the geometry unit.

## Anno's Math Games III
### by Mitsumasa Anno
Philomel Books, 1991

Part 2 of this book, "Exploring Triangles," presents a variety of ways to explore triangles and other shapes and presents ways that triangles are used in the world. Several paper-folding projects are suggested to engage children in exploring shapes.

## A Cloak for the Dreamer
### by Aileen Friedman
### illustrated by Kim Howard
A Marilyn Burns Brainy Day Book, Scholastic, 1994

Three sons work for their father, a tailor. Each son is asked to sew a colorful cloak for the Archduke. The first son sews together rectangles of fabric to make his cloak. The second son sews together squares and then makes a second cloak from triangles. But the third son, a dreamer, uses circles, making a cloak full of holes. The father finds a (geometric) way to fix the dreamer's cloak, and the dreamer gets his wish to go out into the world, taking the cloak with him.

## Eight Hands Round: A Patchwork Alphabet
### by Ann Whitford Paul
HarperCollins Publishers, 1991

This delightful book talks about the importance of patchwork quilts during the first 100 years after the signing of the Declaration of Independence. It shows 26 different patchwork patterns and how the patterns might look sewn together into a quilt. For each design, the book describes aspects of colonial life.

## Grandfather Tang's Story
### by Ann Tompert
Crown Publishers, Inc., 1990

The book opens with Grandfather Tang and Little Soo sitting under a peach tree making different shapes with their tangram pieces. Grandfather Tang tells a story about Chou and Wu Ling, fox fairies who could change their shapes. Each shape is illustrated with a tangram design.

## The Greedy Triangle
### by Marilyn Burns
### illustrated by Gordon Silveria
A Marilyn Burns Brainy Day Book, Scholastic, 1994

A triangle, dissatisfied with only three sides and three angles, goes to a shape-shifter to be changed to a quadrilateral. Life improves, but the shape again becomes unhappy and changes to a pentagon, then a hexagon, a heptagon, and so on, finally learning that being a triangle is best after all.

## The Josefina Story Quilt
### by Eleanor Coerr
Harper and Row, 1986

This book describes the exciting adventures of Josefina as her family moves West in a covered wagon. Josefina makes a patch for each event during their journey. When the family reaches California, Josefina sews the patches together into a story quilt.

## The Keeping Quilt
### by Patricia Polacco
Simon and Schuster, 1993

This book tells a powerful story of a quilt being passed down through four generations of women. The quilt marks important family events—births, weddings, a death—and binds the women together through the years. The baby born at the end symbolizes the continuing connection to future generations.

## The Patchwork Quilt
### by Valerie Flournoy
Dial Books, 1985

Tanya's grandmother begins a quilt made from pieces of the family's old clothes, scraps from a Halloween costume, and a special dress. As Grandma stitches the quilt, Tanya and her mother learn the joys of quilting. When Grandma becomes seriously ill, Tanya takes over work on the quilt. Finally, Grandma is well enough to finish the quilt, which the whole family treasures.

## The Tangram Magician
### by Lisa Campbell Ernst and Lee Ernst
Harry N. Abrams, Inc., 1990

A magician decides to change himself into different creatures. Bold tangram designs depict his transformations. The book invites readers to use the pressure-sensitive vinyl stickers found inside the book to re-create the illustrations and to make their own designs.

# CONTENTS

# HOMEWORK

Homework assignments help extend children's classroom learning and also inform parents about the kinds of activities their children are doing in school. The mathematics instruction that most parents had differs greatly from the learning experiences in this unit. Homework assignments can serve as an effective liaison between school and home.

Three homework assignments are suggested. Each is presented in three parts:

### Homework directions

The directions explain the assignment and include information, when needed, about what students should do to prepare for the assignment.

### The next day

This section gives suggestions for incorporating the students' homework into classroom instruction. It's important for children to know that work they do at home contributes to their classroom learning.

### To parents

A note to parents explains the purpose of the homework and ways they can participate. These communications help parents understand more fully the math instruction their children are getting in school.

# HOMEWORK

## Polygon Search

### Homework directions

The students ask others at home to help them identify 10 objects that are the shape of a polygon or have some part of them that is shaped like a polygon. Children can prepare in class beforehand by identifying polygons in objects in the classroom. Have students record one or two classroom objects on a sheet of paper that they will take home and use for their homework list.

### The next day

Create a class chart with the following labels: Triangles, Quadrilaterals, Pentagons, Hexagons. Working in groups or pairs, children share their findings with one another. When children finish sharing with one another, ask each student to report something for the class chart. The child or the teacher can sketch the item or write its name. (You may need to add more labels if children report heptagons, octagons, nonagons, or decagons.)

### To parents

> Dear Parent,
> Students have learned that polygons are shapes with straight sides that enclose a space and are classified according to the number of sides they have:
>
> | Name of Polygon | Number of Sides |
> | --- | --- |
> | Triangle | 3 |
> | Quadrilateral | 4 |
> | Pentagon | 5 |
> | Hexagon | 6 |
>
> They've also learned that squares, rectangles, parallelograms, and trapezoids are special kinds of quadrilaterals.
> Please help your child identify 10 objects that are the shape of a polygon or have some part of them that is shaped like a polygon. For example, you might notice that your kitchen table is a rectangle or that your house looks like a pentagon from the front. Your child is to record the object you find and the type of polygon.

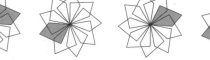

# HOMEWORK

## Homework directions

## The next day

## To parents

# Rotating Designs

Give this assignment after students have made rotating designs in class. The children teach someone at home how to make a rotating design. Have them prepare a tagboard template and take it home along with one or two sheets of drawing paper. Or, you may prefer to give students tagboard and have the people at home cut their own templates. Ask students to bring the designs to school the next day.

Have students share the designs made at home and the templates used to create them. The children report their experiences teaching someone how to make a rotating design, sharing whom they taught and the responses they got. If there is space, students might post the designs and templates on a bulletin board.

Dear Parent,
Making rotating designs is an activity from the geometry unit that integrates art and math and provides the opportunity to discuss the geometry terminology of vertex, perimeter, angle, and rotation. Your child's homework assignment is to teach you how to make a rotating design and to bring the result to class tomorrow.

## HOMEWORK

## Square Up

### Homework directions

Ask the students to teach someone at home to play *Square Up* and to play at least six games. They can take home classroom geoboards and markers or sheets of geoboard dot paper (see Blackline Masters section, page 140) and use two different color markers or crayons.

### The next day

Have children report their experiences playing the game at home, telling with whom they played and the game outcomes.

### To parents

> Dear Parent,
> The game of *Square Up* draws from the mathematical areas of geometry and logic. Playing the game gives children practice with spatial visualization and strategic thinking. Your child's homework assignment is to teach someone at home to play the game and to play at least six games.

# CONTENTS

# BLACKLINE MASTERS

The blackline masters fall into several categories:

### Geometry Menu

This blackline master lists the titles of all the menu activities suggested in the unit. You may choose to enlarge and post this list for a class reference . Some teachers fill in the boxes in front of each title once they have introduced the activity, then students choose activities to do during menu time. Also, some teachers have children copy the list and make check marks or tallies each day to indicate the tasks they worked on; other teachers duplicate the blackline master for each child or pair of students.

### Menu Activities

Six menu activities are included. (Directions for the activities also appear following the Overview section for each menu activity.) You may enlarge and post the menu tasks or make copies for children to use. (Note: A set of classroom posters of the menu activities is available from Cuisenaire Company of America.) Blackline masters for shapes and patterns needed for several activities are also included.

### Recording Sheets

Three blackline masters provide recording sheets for activities. Duplicate an ample supply of each and make copies available to students.

# Geometry Menu

☐ Same and Different

☐ Rotating Designs

☐ Four-Triangle Color Arrangements

☐ The Put-in-Order Problem

☐ Square Up

☐ Covering Boxes

# Same and Different

You need: Two different polygons from
The Four-Triangle Problem

1. Each person chooses a different polygon from
The Four-Triangle Problem.

2. Make two columns on a piece of paper. Label
one "Same" and one "Different."

| Same | Different |
|------|-----------|
|      |           |

3. Describe how the polygons are the same and
different in as many ways as you can.

From *Math By All Means: Geometry, Grades 3–4*   ©1994 Math Solutions Publications

# Rotating Designs

You need: One polygon from The Four-Triangle
Problem
Two sheets of 18-by-24-inch drawing
paper
Tagboard
Scissors
Crayons or markers

1. Choose one of the polygons from The Four-Triangle Problem. Trace it onto tagboard and cut it out. Mark one vertex.

2. Draw a dot in the middle of the sheet of 18-by-24-inch drawing paper. Place the vertex you marked on your tagboard polygon on the dot. Trace around the polygon.

3. Now rotate your polygon. Trace again. Continue rotating and tracing until you return to where you started. Make at least eight rotations. (Be sure to keep the vertex on the dot.) Try to rotate about the same distance each time.

From *Math By All Means: Geometry, Grades 3–4*  ©1994 Math Solutions Publications

# Rotating Designs (page 2)

4. If you'd like, cut out and color your design. Write your name on the back.

5. Make a second rotating design with the same polygon, but using a different vertex.

6. Post your two designs and the tagboard polygon you used. (Don't post the tagboard next to the designs.)

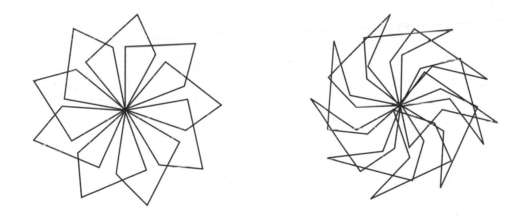

From *Math By All Means: Geometry, Grades 3–4*   ©1994 Math Solutions Publications

# Four-Triangle
# Color Arrangements

P

You need: Polygons from The Four-Triangle Problem
   3-inch paper squares in two colors
   One sheet of 18-by-24-inch newsprint
   Scissors
   Tape or glue

1. Cut one 3-inch square of each color on the diagonal into two triangles.

2. Choose one polygon. Arrange the four triangles to make the polygon you chose. Record your arrangement by taping or gluing your triangles onto newsprint.

3. Cut two more squares into triangles and find another color arrangement for the polygon you chose. Tape or glue it onto the newsprint. Continue cutting and arranging triangles to find all the possible arrangements.

4. Post your work.

# The Put-in-Order Problem

You need: One set of toothpick cards
　　　　　Four toothpicks

1. Arrange your set of toothpick cards so that you can change each design to the next one by moving just one toothpick. Use the four toothpicks to make sure the arrangement works.

2. Record how you solved the problem by listing the card numbers in order.

3. Do this again so you have at least three ways to arrange the cards.

4. Record one of your solutions on the class chart.

Extra: Try to make a continuous loop of your toothpick cards so each changes to the one on either side if one toothpick is moved.

From *Math By All Means: Geometry, Grades 3–4*  ©1994 Math Solutions Publications

# The Put-in-Order
# Problem Samples

This sample of toothpick patterns follows the rule.

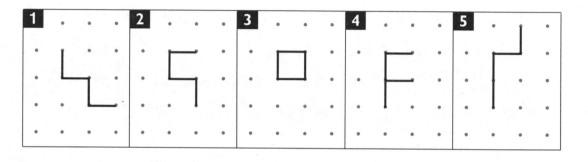

This sample of toothpick patterns does not follow the rule. How can you fix it?

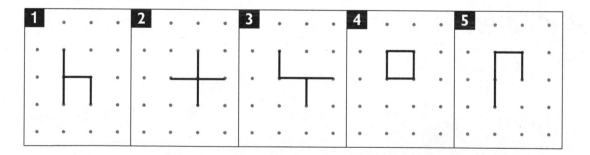

# Square Up

You need: One geoboard
One rubber band
Game markers with holes, 12 each of
two colors
Geoboard dot paper

1. Each player uses a different color marker. Take turns placing a marker on a peg of the geoboard. The object is to place four of your color markers to mark the corners of a square.

2. When you think four of your markers mark the corners of a square, say, "Square Up." The other player says, "Prove it." Prove it by stretching a rubber band around the pegs you think are the corners of a square.

3. If a player has made a square, the game is over. If not, keep playing until one player makes a square or all the pegs are covered.

4. When the game is over, record on geoboard dot paper where you each placed your markers. Play again.

From *Math By All Means: Geometry, Grades 3–4* ©1994 Math Solutions Publications

# Covering Boxes

$\boxed{\text{I}}$

You need: One box
         Construction paper
         Colored yarn in two or three colors
         Glue
         Scissors

1. Glue construction paper to each face of your box. Use the same color for all congruent faces. Try to cover your box neatly.

2. Once you have covered the faces, glue yarn on the edges. Use the same color yarn for edges that are the same length.

From *Math By All Means: Geometry, Grades 3–4*   ©1994 Math Solutions Publications

# Toothpick Dot Paper

From *Math By All Means: Geometry, Grades 3–4*   ©1994 Math Solutions Publications

# Geoboard Dot Paper

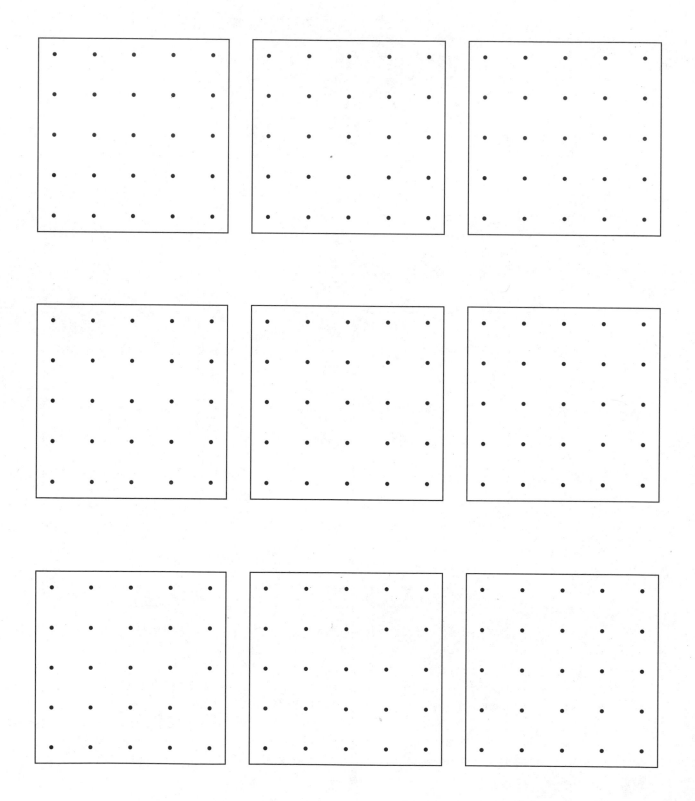

# BIBLIOGRAPHY

**Professional Books and Articles**

Battista, M.T., & Clements, D.H. "A Case for a Logo-Based Elementary School Geometry Curriculum." *Arithmetic Teacher,* 1988: 36(3)

Brooks, J. G. "Constructivists Forging New Connections." *Educational Leadership,* 1990: 47(5), 68–71.

Brown, J. S., Collins, A., & Duguid, P. "Situated Cognition and the Culture of Learning." *Educational Researcher,* 1989: 18(1), 32–42.

Burger, W. F., & Shaughnessy, J. M. "Characterizing the van Hiele Levels of Development in Geometry." *Journal for Research in Mathematics Education,* 1986: 17, 31–48.

Cobb, P., Wood, T., & Yackel, E. "Classrooms as Learning Environments for Teachers and Researchers." In "Constructivist Views on the Teaching and Learning of Mathematics." *Journal for Research in Mathematics Education,* 1990: Monograph No. 4.

Davis, R. B. "The Culture of Mathematics and the Culture of Schools." *The Journal of Mathematical Behavior,* 1989: 8(2), 143–160.

Ethington, C. A., & Wolfle, L. M. "Sex Differences in a Causal Model of Mathematics Achievement." *Journal for Research in Mathematics Education,* 1984: 15, 361–377.

Fuys, D., Geddes, D., & Tischler, R. (Eds.). *English Translation of Selected Writings of Dina van Hiele-Geldof and Pierre M. van Hiele.* Brooklyn College, 1984.

Fuys, D., Geddes, D., & Tischler, R. "The van Hiele Model of Thinking in Geometry Among Adolescents." *Journal for Research in Mathematics Education,* 1988: Monograph No. 3.

Inhelder, B., & Piaget, J. *The Early Growth of Logic in the Child.* Norton, 1964.

Inhelder, B., & Piaget, J. *The Growth of Logical Thinking From Childhood to Adolescence.* Basic Books, 1958.

Labinowicz, E. *The Piaget Primer: Thinking, Learning, Teaching.* Addison-Wesley, 1980.

Lindquist, M. M., & Kouba, V. L. "Geometry." In M. M. Lindquist (Ed.), *Results from the Fourth Mathematics Assessment of the National Assessment of Educational Progress.* National Council of Teachers of Mathematics, 1989.

Mathematical Sciences Education Board. *Reshaping School Mathematics.* National Academy Press, 1989.

Moyer, M. B., & Moyer, J. C. "Ensuring that Practice Makes Perfect: Implications for Children with Learning Difficulties." *Arithmetic Teacher,* 1985: 33(1), 40–42.

National Council of Teachers of Mathematics. *Curriculum and Evaluation Standards for School Mathematics.* NCTM, 1989.

National Council of Teachers of Mathematics. *Professional Standards for Teaching Mathematics.* NCTM, 1991.

National Research Council. *Everybody Counts: A Report to the Nation on the Future of Mathematics Education.* National Academy Press, 1989.

van Hiele, P. M. *Structure and Insight.* Academic Press, 1986.

van Hiele-Geldof, D. *De Didactiek Van In De Eerste Klas Van Het V.H.M.O.* Unpublished doctoral dissertation, University of Utrecht, The Netherlands, 1957. (Translated to English by Fuys, et al., 1984.)

Vygotsky, L. S. *Thought and Language.* M.I.T. Press, 1962.

Vygotsky, L. S. *Mind in Society: The Development of Higher Psychological Processes.* Harvard University Press, 1978.

## Children's Books

Anno, Mitsumasa. *Anno's Math Games III.* Philomel Books, 1991.

*Burns, Marilyn. *The Greedy Triangle.* A Marilyn Burns Brainy Day Book. Scholastic, 1994.

Coerr, Eleanor. *The Josefina Story Quilt.* Harper and Row, 1986.

Ernst, Lisa Campbell, and Lee Ernst. *The Tangram Magician.* Harry N. Abrams, Inc., 1990.

Flournoy, Valerie. *The Patchwork Quilt.* Dial Books, 1985.

*Friedman, Aileen. *A Cloak for the Dreamer.* A Marilyn Burns Brainy Day Book. Scholastic, 1994.

*Paul, Ann Whitford. *Eight Hands Round: A Patchwork Alphabet.* HarperCollins Publishers, 1991.

Polacco, Patricia. *The Keeping Quilt.* Simon & Schuster, 1993.

Tompert, Ann. *Grandfather Tang's Story.* Crown Publishers, Inc., 1990.

## Other Books in the *Math By All Means* Series

*Burns, Marilyn. *Multiplication, Grade 3.* Math Solutions Publications, 1991.

*___. *Place Value, Grades 1–2.* Math Solutions Publications, 1994.

*___. *Probability, Grades 3–4.* Math Solutions Publications, 1995.

*Confer, Chris. *Geometry, Grades 1–2.* Math Solutions Publications, 1994.

*Ohanian, Susan, and Marilyn Burns. *Division, Grades 3–4.* Math Solutions Publications, 1995.

*These books are available from:  Cuisenaire Co. of America, Inc.
P.O. Box 5026
White Plains, NY  10602-5026
(800) 237-3142

# APPENDIX

This appendix presents information about the philosophy of constructivism in general and how the work of Piaget, Vygotsky, and the van Hieles relates to teaching geometry to children. For a selected list of works by these theorists, please see the bibliography on page 141.

## Overview of Constructivism

This geometry unit is based on the instructional philosophy of constructivism. Constructivists believe that we each construct knowledge through our own cognitive acts. We approach understanding as we seek to make sense of our experiences in the world by creating rules that help us explain what we observe. When we make new observations that are inconsistent with the rules we have created, we revise our rules to bring order to our understanding of the world.

Central to a constructivist approach is the idea that children's thinking is qualitatively different from that of adults. A major goal of constructivists is understanding children's thinking.

Applied to teaching, constructivists reject the idea that teachers can pass on knowledge to children and expect that understanding will result. Instead, constructivists believe children develop their own understanding as they reflect upon their own cognitive processes. Therefore, teachers should provide children with experiences that engage them actively in doing, thinking, and reflecting. Also, because not all students think alike, teachers should expect, and respect, variations in students' thinking.

Unlike a behaviorist approach, which values responses instead of thinking processes, a constructivist approach to mathematics has as its goal the child's development of mathematical knowledge. The key issue for teachers is to understand how students interpret what they do, see, and hear rather than how much they can recall.

When the teacher is interested in the process of children's thinking in addition to the product of that thinking, then a shift in the classroom environment and in instructional practices is often necessary. Children benefit from the challenge to explain their thinking and to clarify or rethink their erroneous beliefs.

The job of the teacher, then, becomes one of
- providing a safe and supportive setting in which children feel free to risk being wrong or confused about an idea
- posing challenges and asking students to explain their thinking
- offering support to children as they come up with their own mathematical purposes in place of trying to anticipate where the teacher is going or what he or she wants them to do
- reflecting often and carefully about what students are trying to say about their mathematical understanding.

### Summary of the Work of Jean Piaget

The developmental psychologist Jean Piaget proposed that there are three different kinds of knowledge: logico-mathematical knowledge, physical knowledge, and social knowledge (Inhelder & Piaget, 1958, 1964). Logico-mathematical knowledge is based on relationships. Physical knowledge is based upon experiences with the environment and is derived from manipulating objects and structuring the action internally. While the source of physical knowledge is external, the source of logico-mathematical knowledge is internal. One cannot give or receive knowledge; knowledge must be created in the learner's mind from his or her own experiences.

According to Piaget, social knowledge is based on interactions with and responses from other people. Social knowledge is arbitrary and does not have a logical basis. For example, the convention of where to place the silverware when we set the table or always celebrating Thanksgiving on a Thursday are social conventions. Children acquire social knowledge by interacting with and getting responses from other people.

Understanding the relationships between logico-mathematical, physical, and social knowledge is important to explain why older and younger children respond differently to the same problem. Young children (from birth to approximately age 6) typically have not developed logico-mathematical knowledge, or their logico-mathematical knowledge may take a different form than it will later. Their knowledge sources are primarily physical or social. Children's intellectual development is influenced by their maturation, physical experiences, and social interaction.

According to Piaget, the development of children's intellectual development appears to occur in identifiable stages:

1. *Sensori-motor stage*, characterized by the coordination of physical action (prerepresentational and preverbal); occurs roughly from birth until age 2.

2. *Preoperational stage*, characterized by the ability to represent thought through action and language (prelogical); occurs approximately from age 2 to 7.

3. *Concrete operational stage,* characterized by the ability to mentally reverse actions that previously could only be reversed physically and the ability to hold mentally two or more variables; develops from about age 7 to age 11.

4. *Formal operations stage,* characterized by abstract and unlimited logical thinking; emerges at about age 11.

Disequilibrium is the learning dynamic at each stage. Some sort of external disturbance creates dissonance in the way a child "ordinarily" thinks, triggering disequilibrium. The child responds by assimilating the new experience into his or her existing framework for seeing the world and by accommodating the experience to modify or enrich structures in his or her framework. When the conflict is resolved, the learner returns to a state of balance—or equilibration, as Piaget called it.

## Summary of the Work of Lev Semenovick Vygotsky

The psychologist Lev Semenovick Vygotsky, like Piaget, was interested in mental processes. Vygotsky also viewed learners as constructors of knowledge. However, unlike Piaget, Vygotsky attempted to relate cognitive with social phenomena, believing that social interaction has a significant effect on learning.

Vygotsky distinguished between the child's actual developmental level, which he described as the child's current level of development, and the level of potential development attainable through problem solving with more capable peers or adults. He called the distance between these two levels the zone of proximal development, resulting from the belief that the developmental process lags behind the learning process.

Vygotsky's idea that children are capable of higher levels of development via direct interaction in problem-solving situations with a more capable peer or adult has important implications for instruction. This idea is echoed in the assertion of the NCTM Standards that all students can learn mathematics. No longer appropriate is the model of a child being incapable of learning or deficient in some way.

## Summary of the Work of Pierre van Hiele and Dina van Hiele-Geldof

The Dutch educators Pierre van Hiele and Dina van Hiele-Geldof looked carefully at how children learn about two-dimensional geometry. Their research suggests that children pass through five levels of thinking in geometry (1957/1986). Like Piaget's stages of development, the child passes through each level in sequence. However, it is instruction, not age or biological maturity, that affects the student's progress or lack of it.

The five levels of thinking identified by the van Hieles are:

*Level 0.* The child identifies, names, compares, and operates on geometric figures according to their appearances.

*Level 1.* The child discovers properties and rules of a class of shapes by analyzing components and relationships of components of geometric figures.

*Level 2.* The child makes informal arguments to relate logically properties/rules discovered in Level 1.

*Level 3.* The child uses deduction to prove theorems and discover interrelationships between groups of theorems.

*Level 4.* The child creates, compares, and analyzes theorems in different axiomatic systems.

The levels can be characterized as moving from the concrete (Level 0) to visual (Levels 1–2), to abstract (Levels 3–4). What is implicit at one level becomes explicit at the next.

Pierre van Hiele maintains that each child moves from one level to the next through a five-step process:

1. information, in which the child becomes familiar with the idea;

2. guided orientation, where the child completes tasks that involve looking for different relations among the concept being developed;

3. explicitation, when the child realizes the idea being developed, attempts to express it using words, and learns the appropriate mathematical language for the idea;

4. free orientation, when the child completes more complex activities, exploring other ideas based on what he or she already knows;

5. and integration, in which the student summarizes and reflects on what has been learned (van Hiele, 1957/1984).

The van Hieles believe that children should have opportunities to learn geometry in real-world contexts, physically manipulate objects, be provided with a variety of examples, and see figures represented with multiple orientations. All of these elements are incorporated throughout the activities in this unit.

# INDEX